Yellowstone *to* Yosemite

A storm in the Rockies — Thomas Moran

Yellowstone *to* Yosemite

Early adventures in the mountain West

*Classic adventure-travel
writing
of the early 1870's
with illustrations
by
Thomas Moran
&
other artists of the period*

*Introduced
by Lito Tejada-Flores*

*Western Eye Press
Telluride
1988*

YELLOWSTONE TO YOSEMITE
Early Adventures in the Mountain West
is published by Western Eye Press
Box 917, Telluride, Colorado 81435

This edition © 1988
by Western Eye Press.
All rights reserved.

ISBN 0-941283-01-1
Library of Congress Catalogue Number:
88-50000

The new, non-historical material
in this book was designed and typeset
on a Macintosh computer.
The historical material is printed
from exact photocopies of a rare edition
of Picturesque America,
published in 1872.

Printed in the USA
by Malloy Lithographing

Western Eye Press is a small
Colorado-based publishing adventure
dedicated to publishing handsome,
image-oriented works
on the Rockies and the West,
both historical and original.
Our first title was Linde Waidhofer's
HIGH COLOR,
Spectacular Wildflowers of the Rockies,
a volume of stunning color photography.

Yellowstone to Yosemite

Contents

INTRODUCTION:
The Mountain West in the 1870's
more wilderness than America really wanted

The mountain West — it's still a real place, still magical, still intriguing, still vital after lord knows how many boom-and-bust cycles, how much mining and logging, how much construction and development, how much immigration and tourism. But in the early 1870's, the mountain West was both less and more, much more than it is today. It was less known. And it was wilder. It seemed, and indeed it was, bigger, vaster, richer in mystery and adventure than it seems to us now. The clean-up squads of civilization had scarcely begun chipping away at western mountains, western wilderness.

Americans were just getting used to the idea that there was a country, their own country, "out west" and not merely a frontier. The West in the early 1870's was no longer terra incognita but — after the completion of the trans-continental railroad line in 1868 — a land that could be reached by train in relative comfort, a land that could at last be visited without fear of Indians or outlaws. And of course, then as now, when a blank spot on the map opened up, most people didn't rush to visit it, they rushed to read about it, and better yet, to look at images of the new world. Which is how a book like *Yellowstone to Yosemite* came about — western tales and astonishing illustrations for the armchair travelers of another century.

The five separate journeys that make up this book — journeys through the finest, strangest, strongest scenery in the West — are more than just picturesque travel diaries. They are five trips back through time into vanished regions of the American spirit. The flavor and feeling of the West have certainly changed since the 1870's; but the mountains themselves haven't changed much...we have. Our way of looking at wild country, our reasons for admiring or not admiring it, for exploiting or not exploiting it, for preserving or not preserving wild land in a wild state, have changed again and again.

In this country we have only slowly learned to value wilderness, solitude, the naturalness of nature. Indeed we're still learning. And the five journeys in this book tell us what a long road it's been. At the end of the 19th century, America still had a lot more wilderness than it wanted.

Certainly we aren't the first generation to discover beauty in in the wild open spaces of the West. Early travelers too were awestruck by western mountains, lakes and canyons; and would routinely launch, unblushing, into the most extravagant and overblown descriptions of these "sublime natural wonders." Yet, under the rhetoric, between the lines, one feels another spirit altogether. A discomfort bordering at times on outright fear of so much empty space, so much wildness. A real longing for houses, towns, agriculture and industry. A need, almost visceral, almost universal, at the end of the 19th century to subdue wilderness, to build and transform, to fill this terrible natural vacuum with human works....

Sure enough, they did. Mountains themselves may not change much, but we can graft enough change onto their flanks to totally alter the experience of being in the mountains. And we've done just that. Now that we've finally learned to love it, there isn't much wilderness left in the West.

Fortunately much of the country visited and described in *Yellowstone to Yosemite* was rescued from the fray. When these stories were originally published, Yellowstone had just been named our first National Park. Yosemite, the Grand Canyon, and Rocky Mountain National Park above Estes Park (Chapter Two) came later. Other wonders of the western landscape like the Tahoe Sierra (Chapter Four) were less lucky and some like Glen Canyon (Chapter Three) didn't survive at all.

The contradictions implicit in the 19th century view of the mountain West — admiring the scene without loving the place — were reinforced by extravagant metaphorical descriptions of a West that most Americans hadn't seen, couldn't imagine. Instead of the tangible poetry of things-as-they-are, early traveler/journalists tended to offer their readers vast Wagnerian backdrops for unrealistic flights of fancy, transports of soul.

The stories in this book certainly fall into that category. Although they are all fascinating reading, the actual landscapes are often obscured by a screen of metaphor, a filter of romantic emotions. I first fell in love with these pieces not for their writing but for their wonderful illustrations — Thomas Moran's sketches alone would have been reason enough for reprinting this book. And I only slowly realized how rich and poignant the texts really were. For they show us both an unspoiled West that we've largely lost, and the state of mind that led to its loss.

Lito Tejada-Flores

8

CHAPTER ONE

Our Great National Park
The Valley of the Yellowstone

Welcome to the days before the "good old days." Yellowstone without traffic jams, pre-Winnebago and pre-Kodak, without the phalanxes of zoom lens bracketing the stray moose, the half-tame elk, the dust-caked buffalo and miraculously still inquisitive bear — Yellowstone before any human impact, period. Not the classical Yellowstone of railroad and packtrain, when the word tourist also implied "intrepid," but a Yellowstone so unknown and unvisited that no one but a handful of bona-fide explorers had ever seen it. The days when a journalist, assigned to write a chapter on America's first National Park for a popular travel atlas, wouldn't dream of visiting Yellowstone in person, but instead would only quote the reports of the first survey parties to visit this wilderness basin.

We're fortunate. The "author" of this chapter had little to contribute and didn't, but the man he quotes most extensively, Professor V. F. Hayden was not only the definitive Yellowstone expert of the time, but an impassioned and inspired witness. Hayden's survey work touched nearly every range, subrange and intermontane valley in the Rockies — naming, measuring, mapping, and ultimately influencing a nation's view of its western mountains just as much as the epic romantic landscapes of a Moran or a Bierstadt.

By today's standards Hayden's geological observations are remarkably unsophisticated ("...fragments of rock, and volcanic dust, were poured in unlimited quantities...") but in emotional and aesthetic terms, he got it right. Yellowstone lake really is a vision "worth a lifetime," the Grand Canyon of the Yellowstone really is "decorated with the most brilliant colors that the human eye ever saw." And today, well over a hundred years after Hayden's report provoked Congress into launching the National Park idea, his enthusiasm for this primal western landscape is just as contagious, reads just as well.

Reading this chapter too, one has the strong impression that Congress really didn't know what it was doing when it designated over 3,000 square miles as our first National Park. A good thing too, because if the politicians of the time had been more clear minded about what Yellowstone was, and the precedent they were establishing by setting it aside as a vast natural reserve, they probably would not have done it. It seems clear that Yellowstone became our first National Park less for its strange beauty than because it was considered useless for any "serious" activities like mining or ranching. Since Congress believed there was nothing in Yellowstone worth exploiting, they agreed to preservation. It's a state of mind we like to imagine we've left behind, but which, unfortunately, still haunts public policy in the West today.

L.T-F.

OUR GREAT NATIONAL PARK.

THE VALLEY OF THE YELLOWSTONE.

The Yellowstone.

THE Yellowstone River, one of the tributaries of the Missouri, has a long, devious flow of thirteen hundred miles ere it loses its waters in those of the larger stream. Its source is a noble lake, situated in Wyoming Territory, and nestling amid the snow-peaks of the highest mountain-range in the country. The upper course of the river is through immense cañons and gorges, and its flow is often marked by splendid water-falls and rapids, presenting at various points some of the most remarkable scenery in the country. The entire region about its source is volcanic, and abounds in boiling springs, mud-volcanoes, soda-springs, sulphur-mountains, and geysers the marvels of which outdo those of Iceland.

This remarkable area has recently been set apart by Congress for a great national

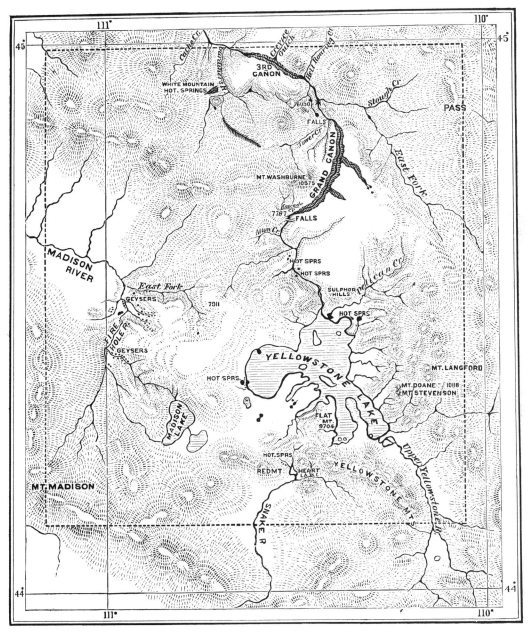

Map of the Yellowstone National Park.

park. It certainly possesses striking characteristics for the purpose to which it has been devoted, exhibiting the grand and magnificent in its snow-capped mountains and dark cañons, the picturesque in its splendid water-falls and strangely-formed rocks, the beautiful in the sylvan shores of its noble lake, and the phenomenal in its geysers, hot springs, and mountains of sulphur. It may be claimed that in no other portion of the globe are there united so many surprising features—none where the conditions of beauty and contrast are so calculated to delight the artist, or where the phenomena are so abundant for the entertainment and instruction of the student.

It is a magnificent domain in its proportions, extending nearly sixty-five miles from north to south, and fifty-five miles from east to west. The Yellowstone Lake lies near the southeasterly corner of the park, the Yellowstone River flowing from its upper boundary, and running almost due north. The lake is twenty-two miles in length, and its average width from ten to fifteen miles. Its height above the level of the sea is seven thousand feet, while its basin is surrounded by mountains reaching an altitude of over ten thousand feet, the peaks of which are covered with perpetual snow. Numerous hot springs are found on the shores of the lake, and also along the banks of the river. About fifteen miles from its source, the river takes two distinct, precipitous leaps, known as the Upper and the Lower Falls, and beyond the falls cuts its way through an immense cañon, the vertical walls of which reach, at places, the height of fifteen hundred feet. Near the western boundary of the park, the Madison, an important tributary of the Columbia, takes its rise; and along one of the branches of this river, known as Fire-Hole River, are found numerous extraordinary geysers, some of which throw volumes of boiling water to a height exceeding two hundred feet. In the northwest corner of the park, the Gallatin, another tributary of the Columbia, takes its rise.

This wonder-land has only recently been explored. For years, marvellous stories have been rife among the hunters of the far West of a mysterious country in the heart of the Rocky Mountains, which the Indians avoided as the abode of the evil spirits, where the rumble of the earthquake is frequently heard, where great jets of steam burst through the earth, where volcanoes throw up mud instead of fire, and where a river flows through gorges of savage grandeur; but beyond these rumors, often apparently absurd exaggerations, nothing was known of that region. An exploring party, under Captain Reynolds, of the United States Engineer Corps, endeavored to enter the Yellowstone Basin in 1859, by way of the Wind-River Mountains, at the south, but failed on account of the ruggedness of the mountains and the depth of the snow. In 1870, an exploring party under General Washburn, escorted by Lieutenant Doane, of the United States Army, succeeded in entering the valley; and from this source the public obtained the first trustworthy accounts of the strange land. Immediately thereafter, an expedition, under sanction of Congress, was organized by the Secretary of the Interior, and placed in the charge of Professor F. V. Hayden, United States geologist; while, at the same time, a party under the command of Lieutenant Barlow, of the United States Engineer Corps, ascended the Yellowstone, and traversed the greater part of the area now included in the park. Professor Hayden's expedition made a thorough exploration of the whole region, and it is to his full and exhaustive report to Congress that we are indebted for an accurate detailed knowledge of the strange features of this remarkable land. It is to this gentleman, probably more than to any other person, that we are indebted for the idea of converting the valley into a national park. The expedition, however, was organized by the Hon. Columbus Delano, Secretary of the Interior; and hence we may attribute the successful issue of the noble conception to the coöperation of the secretary with the purposes of the scientific explorers appointed by him. From the interesting pages of Professor Hayden's report we

Cañon of the Yellowstone.

mainly draw the subjoined particulars of the romantic wonders of our imperial pleasure-ground :

THE YELLOWSTONE BASIN.

"The Yellowstone Basin proper, in which the greater portion of the interesting scenery and wonders is located, comprises only that portion enclosed within the remark-

Gorge of the Yellowstone.

able ranges of mountains which give origin to the waters of the Yellowstone south of Mount Washburn and the Grand Cañon. The range of which Mount Washburn is a conspicuous peak seems to form the north wall, or rim, extending nearly east and west across the Yellowstone, and it is through this portion of the rim that the river has cut its channel, forming the remarkable falls and the still more wonderful cañon. The area of this basin is about forty miles in length. From the summit of Mount Washburn a bird's-eye view of the entire basin may be obtained, with the mountains surrounding it on every side, without any apparent break in the rim. This basin has been called, by some travellers, the vast crater of an ancient volcano. It is probable that during the Pliocene period the entire country drained by the sources of the Yellowstone and the Columbia was the scene of as great volcanic activity as that of any portion of the globe. It might be called one vast crater, made up of thousands of smaller volcanic vents and fissures, out of which the fluid interior of the earth, fragments of rock, and volcanic dust, were poured in unlimited quantities. Hundreds of the nuclei or cores of these volcanic vents are now remaining, some of them rising to a height of ten thousand to eleven thousand feet above the sea. Mounts Doane, Langford, Stevenson, and more than a hundred other peaks, may be seen from any high point on either side of the basin, each of which formed a centre of effusion. Indeed, the hot springs and geysers of this region, at the present time, are nothing more than the closing stages of that wonderful period of volcanic action that began in Tertiary times. In other words, they are the escape-

Column-Rocks.

pipes or vents for those internal forces which once were so active, but are now continually dying out. The evidence is clear that, ever since the cessation of the more powerful volcanic forces, these springs have acted as the escape-pipes, but have continued to decline down to the present time, and will do so in the future, until they cease entirely."

THE FALLS AND THE GRAND CAÑON.

" But the objects of the deepest interest in this region are the falls and the Grand Cañon. I will attempt to convey some idea by a description, but it is only through the eye that the mind can gather any thing like an adequate conception of them. As we approached the margin of the cañon, we could hear the suppressed roar of the falls, resembling distant thunder. The two falls are not more than one-fourth of a mile apart. Above the Upper Falls the Yellowstone flows through a grassy, meadow-like valley, with a calm, steady current, giving no warning, until very near the falls, that it is about to rush over a precipice one hundred and forty feet, and then, within a quarter of a mile, again to leap down a distance of three hundred and fifty feet.

"But no language can do justice to the wonderful grandeur and beauty of the cañon below the Lower Falls; the very nearly vertical walls, slightly sloping down to the water's edge on either side, so that from the summit the river appears like a thread of silver foaming over its rocky bottom; the variegated colors of the sides, yellow, red, brown, white, all intermixed and shading into each other; the Gothic columns of every form, standing out from the sides of the walls with greater variety and more striking colors than ever adorned a work of human art. The margins of the cañon on either side are beautifully fringed with pines. In some places the walls of the cañon are composed of massive basalt, so separated by the jointage as to look like irregular mason-work going to decay. Here and there, a depression in the surface of the basalt has been subsequently filled up by the more modern deposit, and the horizontal strata of sandstone can be seen. The decomposition and the colors of the rocks must have been due largely to hot water from the springs, which has percolated all through, giving to them the present variegated and unique appearance.

"Standing near the margin of the Lower Falls, and looking down the cañon, which looks like an immense chasm or cleft in the basalt, with its sides twelve hundred to fifteen hundred feet high, and decorated with the most brilliant colors that the human eye ever saw, with the rocks weathered into an almost unlimited variety of forms, with here and there a pine sending its roots into the clefts on the sides as if struggling with a sort of uncertain success to maintain an existence—the whole presents a picture that it would be difficult to surpass in Nature. Mr. Thomas Moran, a celebrated artist, and noted for his skill as a colorist, exclaimed, with a kind of regretful enthusiasm, that these beautiful tints were beyond the reach of human art. It is not the depth alone that gives such an impression of grandeur to the mind, but it is also the picturesque forms and coloring. After the waters of the Yellowstone roll over the upper descent, they flow with great rapidity over the apparently flat, rocky bottom, which spreads out to nearly double its width above the falls, and continues thus until near the Lower Falls, when the channel again contracts, and the waters seem, as it were, to gather themselves into one compact mass, and plunge over the descent of three hundred and fifty feet in detached drops of foam as white as snow; some of the large globules of water shoot down like the contents of an exploded rocket. It is a sight far more beautiful than, though not so grand or impressive as, that of Niagara Falls. A heavy mist

THE LOWER FALLS.

always rises from the water at the foot of the falls, so dense that one cannot approach within two hundred or three hundred feet, and even then the clothes will be drenched in a few moments. Upon the yellow, nearly vertical wall of the west side, the mist mostly falls; and for three hundred feet from the bottom the wall is covered with a thick matting of mosses, sedges, grasses, and other vegetation of the most vivid green, which have sent their small roots into the softened rocks, and are nourished by the ever-ascending spray. At the base and quite high up on the sides of the cañon are great quantities of talus, and through the fragments of rocks and decomposed spring deposits may be seen the horizontal strata of breccia."

TOWER CREEK.

"Tower Creek rises in the high divide between the valleys of the Missouri and Yellowstone, and flows about ten miles through a cañon so deep and gloomy that it has very properly earned the appellation of the Devil's Den. As we gaze from the margin down into the depths below, the little stream, as it rushes foaming over the rocks, seems like a white thread, while on the sides of the gorge the sombre pinnacles rise up like Gothic spires. About two hundred yards above its entrance into the Yellowstone, the stream pours over an abrupt descent of one hundred and fifty-six feet, forming one of the most beautiful and picturesque falls to be found in any country. The Tower Falls are about two hundred and sixty feet above the level of the Yellowstone at the junction, and they are surrounded with pinnacle-like columns, composed of the volcanic breccia, rising fifty feet above the falls, and extending down to the foot, standing like gloomy sentinels or like the gigantic pillars at the entrance of some grand temple. One could almost imagine that the idea of the Gothic style of architecture had been caught from such carvings of Nature. Immense bowlders of basalt and granite here obstruct the flow of the stream above and below the falls; and, although, so far as we can see, the gorge seems to be made up of the volcanic cement, yet we know that, in the loftier mountains, near the source of the stream, true granitic as well as igneous rocks prevail."

YELLOWSTONE LAKE.

"On the 28th of July (1871)," says Professor Hayden, "we arrived at the lake, and pitched our camp on the northwest shore, in a beautiful grassy meadow or opening among the dense pines. The lake lay before us, a vast sheet of quiet water, of a most delicate ultramarine hue, one of the most beautiful scenes I have ever beheld. The entire party were filled with enthusiasm. The great object of all our labors had been reached, and we were amply paid for all our toils. Such a vision is worth a lifetime, and only one of such marvellous beauty will ever greet human eyes. From whatever point of view one may behold it, it presents a unique picture. We had brought up the

CLIFFS ON THE YELLOWSTONE.

framework of a boat, twelve feet long and three and a half feet wide, which we covered with stout ducking, well tarred. On the morning of the 29th, Messrs. Stevenson and Elliott started across the lake in the Anna, the first boat ever launched on the Yellowstone, and explored the nearest island, which we named after the principal assistant of the expedition, who was undoubtedly the first white man that ever placed foot upon it. Our little bark, whose keel was the first to plough the waters of the most beautiful lake on our continent, and which must now become historical, was named by Mr. Stevenson in compliment to Miss Anna L. Dawes, the amiable daughter of Hon. H. L. Dawes. My whole party were glad to manifest, by this slight tribute, their gratitude to the distinguished statesman, whose generous sympathy and aid had contributed so much toward securing the appropriation which enabled them to explore this marvellous region.

"Usually in the morning the surface of the lake is calm, but, toward noon and after, the waves commence to roll, and the white caps rise high, sometimes four or five feet. Our little boat rode the waves well; but, when a strong breeze blew, the swell was too great, and we could only venture along the shore. This lake is about twenty-two miles in length from north to south, and an average of ten to fifteen miles in width from east to west. It has been aptly compared to the human hand; the northern portion would constitute the palm, while the southern prolongations or arms might represent the fingers. There are some of the most beautiful shore-lines along this lake that I ever saw. Some of the curves are as perfect as if drawn by the hand of art. Our little boat performed most excellent service. A suitable framework was fastened in the stern for the lead and line, and, with the boat, a system of soundings was made that gave a very fair idea of the average depth of the lake. The greatest depth discovered was three hundred feet. It is fed by the snows that fall upon the lofty ranges of mountains that surround it on every side. The water of the lake has at all seasons nearly the temperature of cold spring-water. The most accomplished swimmer could live but a short time in it; the dangers attending the navigation of such a lake in a small boat are thereby greatly increased. The lake abounds in salmon-trout, and is visited by great numbers of wild-fowl.

"We adopted the plan of making permanent camps at different points around the lake while explorations of the country in the vicinity were made. Our second camp was pitched at the hot springs on the southwest arm. This position commanded one of the finest views of the lake and its surroundings. While the air was still, scarcely a ripple could be seen on the surface, and the varied hues, from the most vivid green shading to ultramarine, presented a picture that would have stirred the enthusiasm of the most fastidious artist. Sometimes, in the latter portion of the day, a strong wind would arise, arousing this calm surface into waves like the sea. Near our camp there is a thick deposit of the silica, which has been worn by the waves into a bluff wall, twenty-five feet high above the water. It must have originally extended far out into the lake. The belt of springs at this place is about three miles long and half a mile wide. The deposit now can be seen far out in the deeper portions of the lake, and the bubbles that arise to the surface in various places indicate the presence, at the orifice, of a hot spring beneath. Some of the funnel-shaped craters extend out so far into the lake, that the members of our party stood upon the silicious mound, extended the rod into the deeper waters, and caught the trout, and cooked them in the boiling spring, without removing them from the hook. These orifices, or chimneys, have no connection with the waters of the lake. The hot fumes coming up through fissures, extending down toward the interior of the earth, are confined within the walls of the orifice, which are mostly circular, and beautifully lined with delicate porcelain."

THE HOT SPRINGS.

"Upon the west side of Gardiner's River, on the slope of the mountain, is one of the most remarkable groups of hot springs in the world. The springs in action at the present time are not very numerous, or even so wonderful as

Tower Creek.

some of those higher up in the Yellowstone Valley or in the Fire-Hole Basin, but it is in the remains that we find so instructive records of their past history. The calcareous deposits from these springs cover an area of about two miles square. The active springs extend from the margin of the river five thousand five hundred and forty-five feet, to an elevation nearly one thousand above, or six thousand five hundred and twenty-two feet above the sea by barometrical measurement. Our path led up the hill by the side of a wall of lower cretaceous rocks, and we soon came to the most abundant remains of old springs, which, in past times, must have been very active. The steep hill, for nearly a mile, is covered with a thick crust, and, though much decomposed and covered with a moderately thick growth of pines and cedars, still bore traces of the same wonderful architectural beauty displayed in the vicinity of the active springs farther up the hill. After ascending the side of the mountain, about a mile above the channel of Gardiner's River, we suddenly came in full view of one of the finest displays of Nature's architectural skill the world can produce. The snowy whiteness of the deposit at once suggested the name of White-Mountain Hot Spring. It had the appearance of a frozen cascade. If a group of springs near the summit of a mountain were to distribute their waters down the irregular declivities, and they were slowly congealed, the picture would bear some resemblance in form. We pitched our camp at the foot of the principal mountain, by the side of the stream that contained the aggregated waters of the hot springs above, which, by the time they had reached our camp, were sufficiently cooled for our use. Before us was a hill two hundred feet high, composed of the calcareous deposit of the hot springs, with a system of step-like terraces, which would defy any description by words. The eye alone could convey any adequate conception to the mind. The steep sides of the hill were ornamented with a series of semicircular basins, with margins varying in height from a few inches to six or eight feet, and so beautifully scalloped and adorned with a kind of bead-work, that the beholder stands amazed at this marvel of Nature's handiwork. Add to this a snow-white ground, with every variety of shade, of scarlet, green, and yellow, as brilliant as the brightest of our aniline dyes. The pools or basins are of all sizes, from a few inches to six or eight feet in diameter, and from two inches to two feet deep. As the water flows from the spring over the mountain-side from one basin to another, it loses continually a portion of its heat, and the bather can find any desirable temperature. At the top of the hill there is a broad, flat terrace, covered more or less with these basins, one hundred and fifty to two hundred yards in diameter, and many of them going to decay. Here we find the largest, finest, and most active spring of the group at the present time. The largest spring is very near the outer margin of the terrace, and is twenty-five by forty feet in diameter, the water so perfectly transparent that one can look down into the beautiful ultramarine depth to the bottom of the basin. The sides of the basin are ornamented with coral-like forms, with a great variety of shades, from pure white to a bright cream-yellow, and the blue sky, reflected in the

TOWER FALLS.

Yellowstone Lake.

transparent waters, gives an azure tint to the whole, which surpasses all art. Underneath the sides of many of these pools are rows of stalactites, of all sizes, many of them exquisitely ornamented, formed by the dripping of the water over the margins of the basins.

"On the west side of this deposit, about one-third of the way up the White Mountain from the river and terrace, which was once the theatre of many active springs, old chimneys, or craters, are scattered thickly over the surface, and there are several large holes and fissures leading to vast caverns beneath the crust. The crust gives off a dull, hollow sound beneath the tread, and the surface gives indistinct evidence of having been adorned with the beautiful pools or basins just described. As we pass up to the base of the principal terrace,-we find a large area covered with shallow pools, some of them containing water, with all the ornamentations perfect, while others are fast going to decay, and the decomposed sediment is as white as snow. Upon this kind of sub-terrace is a remarkable cone, about fifty feet in height, and twenty feet in diameter at the base. From its form we gave it the name of the Liberty Cap. It is undoubtedly the remains of an extinct geyser. The water was forced up with considerable power, and probably without intermission, building up its own crater until the pressure beneath was exhausted, and then it gradually closed itself over at the summit and perished. No water flows from it at the present time. The layers of lime were deposited around it like the layers of straw on a thatched roof, or hay on a conical stack.

"The entire Yellowstone Basin is covered more or less with dead and dying springs, but there are centres or groups where the activity is greatest at the present time. Below the falls there is an extensive area covered with the deposits which extend from the south side of Mount Washburn across the Yellowstone rim, covering an area of ten or fifteen square miles. On the south side of Mount Washburn there is quite a remarkable group of active springs. They are evidently diminishing in power, but the rims all around reveal the most powerful manifestations far back in the past. Sulphur, copper, alum, and soda, cover the surface. There is also precipitated around the borders of some of the mud-springs a white efflorescence, probably nitrate of potash. These springs are located on the side of the mountain nearly one thousand feet above the margin of the cañon, but extend along into the level portions below. In the immediate channel of the river, at the present time, there are very few springs, and these not important. A few small steam-vents can be observed only from the issue of small quantities of steam. One of these springs was bubbling quite briskly, but had a temperature of only one hundred degrees. Extending across the cañon on the opposite side of the Yellowstone, interrupted here and there, this group of springs extends for several miles, forming one of the largest deposits of silica, but only here and there are there signs of life. Many of the dead springs are mere basins, with a thick deposit of iron on the sides, lining the channel of the water that flows from them. These vary in temperature from ninety-eight to one hundred and twenty degrees. The highest temperature was one hundred and ninety-two degrees. The steam-vents are very numerous, and the chimneys are lined with sulphur. Where the crust can be removed, we find the under-side lined with the most delicate crystals of sulphur, which disappear like frost-work at the touch. Still there is a considerable amount of solid amorphous sulphur. The sulphur and the iron, with the vegetable matter, which is always very abundant about the springs, give, through the almost infinite variety of shades, a most pleasing and striking picture."

MUD-SPRINGS.

"We pitched our camp on the shore of the river, near the Mud Springs, thirteen and a half miles above our camp on Cascade Creek. The springs are scattered along on both sides of the river, sometimes extending upon the hill-sides fifty to two hundred feet above the level of the river. Commencing with the lower or southern side of the group, I will attempt to describe a few of them. The first one is a remarkable mud-spring, with a well-defined circular rim composed of fine clay, and raised about four feet above the surface around, and about six feet above the mud in the basin. The diameter of the basin is about eight feet. The mud is so fine as to be impalpable, and the whole may be most aptly compared to a caldron of boiling mush. The gas is constantly escaping, throwing up the mud from a few inches to six feet in height ; and there is no doubt that there are times when it is hurled out ten to twenty feet, accumulating around the

The First Boat on the Yellowstone.

rim of the basin. About twenty yards distant from the mud-spring just described is a second one, with a basin nearly circular, forty feet in diameter, the water six or eight feet below the margin of the rim. The water is quite turbid, and is boiling moderately. Small springs are flowing into it from the south side, so that the basin forms a sort of reservoir. The temperature, in some portions of the basin, is thus lowered to ninety-eight degrees. Several small hot springs pour their surplus water into it, the temperatures of which are one hundred and eighty, one hundred and seventy, one hundred and eighty-four, and one hundred and fifty-five degrees. In the reservoirs, where the water boils up with considerable force, the temperature is only ninety-six degrees, showing that the bubbling was due to the escape of gas. The bubbles stand all over the surface. About twenty feet from the last is a small mud-spring, with an orifice ten inches in diameter, with whitish-brown mud, one hundred and eighty-two degrees. Another basin near the last has two orifices, the one throwing out the mud with a dull thud about once in three seconds, spurting the mud out three or four feet; the other is content to boil up quite violently, occasionally throwing the mud ten to twelve inches. This mud, which has been wrought in these caldrons for perhaps hundreds of years, is so fine and pure that the manufacturer of porcelain-ware would go into ecstasy at the sight. The

Hot-Spring Cone.

contents of many of the springs are of such a snowy whiteness that, when dried in cakes in the sun or by a fire, they resemble the finest meerschaum. The color of the mud depends upon the superficial deposits which cover the ground, through which the waters of the springs reach the surface. They were all clear hot springs originally, perhaps geysers even; but the continual caving-in of the sides has produced a sort of mud-pot, exactly the same as the process of preparing a kettle of mush. The water is at first clear and hot; then it becomes turbid from the mingling of the loose earth around the sides of the orifice, until, by continued accessions of earth, the contents of the basin become of the consistency of thick mush, and, as the gas bursts up through it, the dull, thud-like noise is produced. Every possible variation of condition of the contents is

Hot Springs.

found, from simple milky turbidness to a stiff mortar. On the east side of the Yellowstone, close to the margin of the river are a few turbid and mud springs, strongly impregnated with alum. The mud is quite yellow, and contains much sulphur. This we called a mud-sulphur spring. The basin is fifteen by thirty feet, and has three centres of ebullition, showing that, deep down underneath the superficial earth, there are three separate orifices, not connected with each other, for the emission of heated waters."

SULPHUR-MOUNTAIN AND MUD-VOLCANO.

From Lieutenant Barlow's report we derive the following description of a sulphur-mountain near Cascade Creek, and of a mud-volcano a few miles distant: " Toward the western verge of a prairie of several miles in extent, above the Yellowstone Falls, a hill of white rock was discovered, which, upon investigation, proved to be another of the ' soda-mountains,' as they are called by the hunters. Approaching nearer, I found jets of smoke and steam issuing from the face of the hill, while its other side was hollowed out into a sort of amphitheatre, whose sides were steaming with sulphur-fumes, the ground hot and parched with internal fires. Acre after acre of this hot volcanic surface lay before me, having numerous cracks and small apertures, at intervals of a few feet, whence were expelled, sometimes in steady, continuous streams, sometimes in puffs, like those from an engine, jets of vapor more or less impregnated with mineral substances. I ascended the hill, leaving my horse below, fearful that he might break through the thin rock-crust, which in many places gave way beneath the tread, revealing caverns of pure crystallized sulphur, from which hot fumes were sure to issue. The crystals were very fine, but too frail to transport without the greatest care. A large boiling spring, emitting strong fumes of sulphur and sulphuretted hydrogen, not at all agreeable, was also found. The water from this spring, overrunning its basin, trickled down the hill-side, leaving a highly-colored trace in the chalky rock. Upon the opposite side was found a number of larger springs. One, from its size and the power it displayed in throwing water to the height of several feet above the surface, was worthy of notice. Near this was a spring having regular pulsations, like a steam-engine, giving off large quantities of steam, which would issue forth with the roar of a hurricane. This was, in reality, a steam-volcano ; deep vibrations in the subterraneous caverns, extending far away beneath the hill, could be distinctly heard.

"The country from this point to the mud-volcano, a few miles above, was mostly rolling prairie, intersected with several streams flowing into the river, some of them having wide estuaries and adjacent swampy flats, covered with thick marsh-grass. Ducks were usually found in these sluggish streams, as well as in the little lakes so numerous throughout this whole region. We camped on the bank of the river, in the immediate vicinity of the mud-geyser. This being the first specimen of the true geysers yet seen, it was examined with great curiosity. The central point of interest, however, is the mud-volcano, which has broken out from

Liberty-Cap.

the side of a well-timbered hill. The crater is twenty-five feet across at the top, gradually sloping inward to the bottom, where it becomes about half this diameter. Its depth is about thirty feet. The deposit is gray mud, nearly pure alumina, and has been thrown up by the action of the volcano at no very distant period. The rim of the crater on the down-hill side is some ten feet in height, and trees fifty

Mud-Springs.

feet high and a hundred feet distant are loaded with mud thrown from this volcano. The surface of the bottom is in a constant state of ebullition, puffing and throwing up masses of boiling mud, and sending forth dense columns of steam several hundred feet above the surrounding forests. This vapor can be seen for many miles in all directions. Some four hundred yards from this crater are three large hot springs of muddy water, one of which proved to be a geyser, having periods of active eruption about every six hours. The phenomena attending these eruptions are as follows: Soon after the violent period passes, the water in the pool gradually subsides through the orifice in the centre, the surface falling several feet, the water almost entirely disappearing from sight. It then gradually rises again until the former level is reached, during which occasional ebullitions of greater or lesser magnitude occur. Great agitation then ensues; pulsations, at regular intervals of a few seconds, take place, at each of which the water in the crater is elevated higher and higher, until, finally, after ten minutes, a column is forced up to the height of thirty or forty feet. During this period waves dash against the sides of the basin, vast clouds of steam escape, and a noise like the rumbling of an earthquake takes place. Suddenly, after about fifteen minutes of this commotion, the waves recede, quiet is restored, the waters sink gradually to their lowest limit, from which they soon rise again, and repeat the same operation."

Soda-Springs.

THE GREAT GEYSER BASIN.

We also quote from Lieutenant Barlow's report the following account of the great Geysers on Fire-Hole River: " Entering the basin from the north, and following the banks of the Fire-Hole River, whose direction there is about northeast, a series of rapids, quite near together, is encountered, when the river makes a sharp bend to the southwest, at which point is found a small steam-jet upon the right. A warm stream comes in from the left, falling over a bank ten feet in height. A short distance beyond a second rapid is found, and then another, about one hundred yards farther on, where the gate of the Geyser Basin is entered. Here, on either side of the river, are two lively geysers called the Sentinels. The one on the left is in constant agitation, its waters revolving horizontally with great violence, and occasionally spouting upward to the height of twenty feet, the lateral direction being fifty feet. Enormous masses of steam are ejected. The crater of this geyser is three feet by ten. The opposite Sentinel is not so constantly active, and is smaller. The rapids here are two hundred yards in length, with a fall of thirty feet. Following the bank of the river, whose

THE GIANT GEYSER.

general course is from the southeast, though with many windings, two hundred and fifty yards from the gate we reach three geysers acting in concert. When in full action, the display from these is very fine. The waters spread out in the shape of a fan, in consequence of which they have been named the Fan Geysers. A plateau, opposite the latter, contains fifteen hot springs, of various characteristics; some are of a deep-blue color, from sulphate of copper held in solution, and having fanciful caverns distinctly visible below the surface of the water. The openings at the surface are often beautifully edged with delicately-wrought fringes of scalloped rock. One variety deposits a red or brown leathery substance, partially adhering to the sides and bottom of the cavern, and waving to and fro in the water like plants. The size of these springs varies from five to forty feet in diameter. One hundred yards farther up the east side of the stream is found a double geyser, a stream from one of its orifices playing to the height of eighty or ninety feet, emitting large volumes of steam. From the formation of its crater it was named the Well Geyser. Above is a pine-swamp of cold water, opposite which, and just above the plateau previously mentioned, are found some of the most interesting and beautiful geysers of the whole basin.

" First we come upon two smaller geysers near a large spring of blue water, while a few yards beyond are seen the walls and arches of the Grotto. This is an exceedingly intricate formation, eight feet in height, and ninety in circumference. It is hollowed into fantastic arches, with pillars and walls of almost indescribable variety. This geyser plays to the height of sixty feet several times during twenty-four hours. The water, as it issues from its numerous apertures, has a very striking and picturesque effect.

" Near the Grotto is a large crater, elevated four feet above the surface of the hill, having a rough-shaped opening, measuring two by two and a half feet. Two hundred yards farther up are two very fine large geysers, between which and the Grotto are two boiling springs. Proceeding one hundred and fifty yards farther, and passing two hot springs, a remarkable group of geysers is discovered. One of these has a huge crater five feet in diameter, shaped something like the base of a horn—one side broken down— the highest point being fifteen feet above the mound on which it stands. This proved to be a tremendous geyser, which has been called the Giant. It throws a column of water the size of the opening to the measured altitude of one hundred and thirty feet, and continues the display for an hour and a half. The amount of water discharged was immense, about equal in quantity to that in the river, the volume of which, during the eruption, was doubled. But one eruption of this geyser was observed. Its periodic turns were not, therefore, determined. Another large crater close by has several orifices, and, with ten small jets surrounding it, formed, probably, one connected system. The hill built up by this group covers an acre of ground, and is thirty feet in height."

In the report to Congress by the Committee on Public Lands we learn that "the entire area comprised within the limits of the reservation is not susceptible of cultivation with any degree of certainty, and the winters would be too severe for stock-raising. Whenever the altitude of the mountain-districts exceeds six thousand feet above tide-water, their settlement becomes problematical, unless there are valuable mines to attract people. The entire area within the limits of the proposed reservation is over six thousand feet in altitude; and the Yellowstone Lake, which occupies an area fifteen by twenty-two miles, or three hundred and thirty square miles, is seven thousand four hundred and twenty-seven feet. The ranges of mountains that hem the valleys in on every side rise to the height of ten thousand and twelve thousand feet, and are covered with snow all the year. These mountains are all of volcanic origin, and it is not probable that any mines or minerals of value will ever be found there. During the months of June, July, and August, the climate is pure and most invigorating, with scarcely any rain or storms of any kind; but the thermometer frequently sinks as low as twenty-six degrees. There is frost every month of the year." These statements make it evident that, in setting apart this area "as a great national park and pleasure-ground for the benefit and enjoyment of the people," no injury has been done to other interests. The land did not need to be purchased, but simply withdrawn from "settlement, occupancy, or sale;" and hence, by timely action, a great public benefit was secured, which in a few years would have been impracticable, or at least attainable only with great difficulty. The time is not distant, in the opinion of the Congressional committee, when this region will be a place of "resort for all classes of people from all portions of the globe." The Northern Pacific Railroad, now rapidly advancing toward completion, will render the park easily accessible; and, this once accomplished, the marvels of the strange domain will tempt the curious in great numbers to visit it. As a place of resort for invalids, the Yellowstone Valley, on account of its pure and exhilarating atmosphere, is believed to be unexcelled by any portion of the globe; and, if this anticipation prove true, there will be additional reason to be gratified at the wise forethought which secured it for public uses forever. The Congressional enactment which creates the park amply provides for its control and management. "It shall," says the act, "be under the exclusive control of the Secretary of the Interior, whose duty it shall be, as soon as practicable, to make and publish such rules and regulations as he may deem necessary or proper for the care and management of the same. Such regulations shall provide for the preservation, from injury or spoliation, of all timber, mineral deposits, natural curiosities, or wonders, within said park. The secretary may, in his discretion, grant leases for building-purposes, for terms not exceeding ten years, of small parcels of ground, at such places in said park as shall require the erection of buildings for the accommodation of visitors; all of the proceeds of said leases to be expended under his direction in the management of the same, and the construction of roads and bridle-paths therein."

CHAPTER TWO

The Rocky Mountains
Across Colorado in the footsteps of the Hayden survey

Today when we think "mountains," some of us think "playground," others "paradise," but no one shivers with apprehension or dread. Yet it wasn't always the case. Modern Americans escape to the mountains — and when they can, to the still intact wilderness zones of the Rockies and other ranges — with something like glee, excitement and delight. We hike across a rugged crest and look down into an uninhabited alpine valley with a sense of privilege and wonder. And the idea that, high and alone in the Rockies, we might be overwhelmed with nostalgia for farmhouses and white picket fences seems totally absurd.

It didn't seem at all absurd to W. H. Rideing, the author of this chapter, who is constantly torn between honest admiration of mountain grandeur and an equally honest distaste for harsh, "empty," untamed landscapes — a distaste that sometimes borders on fear and repulsion. ("Ah, that we might never be left alone to hear the secret voice and dread revelations of these magnificent spaces!") The unease that mountain wilderness provoked in so many early travelers sometimes becomes outright paranoia. ("...two or three conies snarl at us...") And sometimes it melts away in the most extravagant praise.

Even though written with an ambiguous and grudging enthusiasm, this picture of the late 19th-century Rockies is a rich one. Rideing too, uses the ubiquitous Hayden survey to give structure to his tale of rambles through Colorado's highest peaks. But rather than quoting survey reports, he creates a fanciful and somewhat impractical itinerary through most of the mountain districts that the Hayden party surveyed. In the text we can recognize mountains we love seen through altogether different eyes... But in Thomas Moran's illustrations all ambiguity disappears; these are romantic yet strikingly accurate portraits of mountains that can only attract, only enchant.

L.T-F.

THE ROCKY MOUNTAINS.

WITH ILLUSTRATIONS BY THOMAS MORAN.

IN a general and some-what indistinct way, we may all claim to know something about the Rocky Mountains, and we all remember the reverence and awe their name inspired in our school-days; but our mature knowledge of them is neither exact nor extensive. Perhaps we have heard of Pike's Peak, Gray's Peak, and Long's Peak; but we are hazy as to their altitudes and characteristics, and could much more easily answer questions about the Alps, the Andes, or the Himalayas,

Tower Rock, Garden of the Gods.

LONG'S PEAK, FROM ESTE'S PARK.

than about the magnificent chain that embraces an area of sixty thousand square miles in Colorado alone, and nurtures the streams that pour their volume into the greatest and most widely separate oceans. We may have crossed the continent in the iron pathway of the Union Pacific over and over again, and not seen to advantage one of the peaks that cluster and soar to almost incomparable elevations—minor hills hiding them from the travellers in the cars; and we may be inclined to think less of the main range than of the Sierra Nevadas, because the railway has shown us the greatest beauties of the latter. But there is not a false pretence about them; no writer has exaggerated in extolling their grandeur, nor even adequately described it.

The chain is a continuation northward of the Cordilleras of Central America and Mexico. From Mexico it continues through the States and Territories lying between the Pacific and the head-waters of the streams that flow into the Mississippi, spreading over an area of one thousand miles from east to west. Still inclining northward, and still broken into several ranges, it passes into the British possessions to the north, the eastern range reaching the Arctic Ocean in about latitude 70° north, and the western passing near the coast, and ending near Prince William's Sound, where Mount St. Elias, in latitude 60°, stands upon the borders of the Pacific, at the height of seventeen thousand eight hundred feet above the sea-level.

We do not like the word "Backbone" applied to the mountains. Let us rather call them the Snow-Divide of the continent, or, as the main range is sometimes named, the Mother-Sierras. Occasionally, too, they are called the Alps of America by one of those absurd whims of literary nomenclature that insist upon calling New Orleans the Paris of America, Saratoga the Wiesbaden of America, and Lake George the Windermere of America, just as though we had nothing distinctly our own, and Nature had simply duplicated her handiwork across the seas in creating the present United States. The Rocky Mountains are not like the Alps, and in some things they surpass them. From the summit of Mount Lincoln, near Fairplay, Colorado, on a clear day, such a view is obtained as you cannot find on the highest crests of the Swiss mountains. In the rear, and in the front, the peaks ascend so thickly that Nature seems to have here striven to build a dividing wall across the universe. There are one hundred and thirty of them not less than thirteen thousand feet high, or within less than three thousand feet of Mont Blanc; and at least fifty over fourteen thousand feet high. Almost below the dome on which we stand, we can see a low ridge across a valley, separating the river Platte, leading to the Gulf of Mexico, and the Blue River, leading to the Gulf of California. On one side are the famous Gray's and Evans's Peaks, scarcely noticeable among a host of equals; Long's Peak is almost hidden by the narrow ridge; Pike's is very distinct and striking. Professor Whitney has very truly said, and we have repeated, that no such view as this is to be obtained in Switzerland, either for reach or the magnificence of the included heights. Only in the Andes or Himalayas might

BOWLDER CAÑON.

we see its equal. But it is also true that one misses the beauty of the pure Alpine mountains, with the glaciers streaming down their sides. The snow lies abundantly in lines, and banks, and masses; yet it covers nothing.

Even among eminent scientific men there has been a dense ignorance about the Rocky Mountains, and especially about the heights of the several peaks. Until 1873,

Frozen Lake, Foot of James's Peak.

only small areas of our vast Territories had been surveyed and accurately mapped. The greater space had been unnoticed, and uncared for. But in that year a geological and geographical survey of Colorado was made, under the able direction of Dr. F. V. Hayden; and the results have exceeded all expectations. The position of every leading peak in thirty thousand square miles was fixed last summer, including the whole region between parallels 38° and 40° 20′ north, and between the meridians 104° 30′ and 107° west. The ground was divided into three districts, the northern district including the Middle Park, the middle district including the South Park, and the southern district the San-Luis Park. In these three districts the range reveals itself as one of the grandest in the world, reaching its greatest elevations, and comprising one of the most interesting areas

Gray's Peak.

on the continent. As unscientific persons, we owe Professor Hayden a debt of gratitude for reassuring us that the Rocky Mountains are all our forefathers thought them, and not mythical in their splendors. How much more the *savants* owe him, we will not venture to say. We ought to add, however, that he was singularly fortunate in unearthing, so to speak, the most representative scenery, as the photographs made attest; and present or prospective travellers cannot do better than follow in the footsteps of his expedition, as we mean to do in this article.

Early in May we are far north, with a detachment of the Hayden expedition, encamped in the Estes Park, or Valley. Park, by-the-way, is used in these regions as a sort of variation on the sweeter-sounding word. The night is deepening as we pitch our tents. We are at the base of Long's Peak — about half-way between Denver City and the boundary-line of Wyoming — and can only dimly see its clear-cut outline and graceful crests, as the last hues of sunset fade and depart. Supper consoles us after our long day's march; we retire to our tents, but are not so exhausted that we cannot make merry. In this lonely little valley, with awful chasms and hills around, in a wilderness of glacier creation, scantily robed with dusky pine and hemlock, the hearty voice of our expedition breaks many slumbering echoes in the chilly spring night. A void is filled. A man on the heights, looking into the valley, would be conscious of a change in the sentiment of the scene. The presence of humanity infuses itself into the inanimate. It is so all through the region. Alone, we survey the magnificent reaches of mountain, hill-side, and plain, with a subdued spirit, as on the brink of a grave. Our sympathies find vent, but not in hysterical adulation. Our admiration and wonder are mingled with a degree of awe that restrains expression. It would be much more easy to go into ecstasies over the home-like view from the summit of Mount Washington than over peaks that are more than twice as high, and incomparably grander. There are brightness and life, smooth pastures and pretty houses, on the New-England mountain. Out here there are waste, ruggedness, and sombre colors. The heart of man is not felt; we gaze at the varied forms, all of them massive, most of them beautiful, feeling ourselves in a strange world. The shabby hut of the squatter, and straggling mining-camp, deep set in a ravine, are an inexpressible relief; and so our white tents, erected on the fertile acres of the Estes Park, throw a gleam of warmth among the snowy slopes, and impart to the scene that something without which the noblest country appears dreary, and awakens whatever latent grief there is in our nature.

Betimes in the morning we are astir, and the full glory of the view bursts upon us. The peak is the most prominent in the front range, soaring higher than its brothers around; and we have seen it as we approached from the plains. It is yet too early in the season for us to attempt the ascent; the snow lies more than half-way down; but from this little valley, where our tents are pitched, we have one of the finest views possible. The slopes are gentle and almost unbroken for a considerable distance; but, reaching higher, they terminate in sharp, serrated lines, edged with a ribbon of silver light. The snow is not distributed evenly. In some places it lies thick, and others are only partly covered by streaky, map-like patches, revealing the heavy color of the ground and rock beneath. A range of foot-hills of clumsy contour leads the way to the peaks which mount behind them. The park is a lovely spot, sheltered, fertile, and wooded. It

SUMMIT OF GRAY'S PEAK.

is an excellent pasture for large herds of cattle, and is used for that purpose. A few families are also settled here; and, as the valley is the only practicable route for ascending the peak, it is destined, no doubt, to become a stopping-place for future tourists. It is seven thousand seven hundred and eighty-eight feet above the level of the sea, and six thousand three hundred feet below Long's Peak, which is said to be about fourteen thousand and eighty-eight feet high. The peak is composed of primitive rock, twisted and torn into some of the grandest cañons in this famed country of cañons. While we remain here, we are constantly afoot. The naturalists of the expedition are overjoyed at their good fortune, and the photographers are alert to catch all they can while the light lasts. The air is crisp, joyous, balsamic. Ah! that we might never be left alone to hear the secret voice and the dread revelations of these magnificent spaces! But it follows us, and oppresses us; and we are never safe from its importunities without a mirthful, unimpressionable companion. It is a terrible skeleton in the closet of the mountain, and it comes forth to fill us with dismay and grief.

Soon we are on the march again, tramping southward through stilly valleys, climbing monstrous bowlders, fording snow-fed streams, mounting perilous heights, descending awful chasms. Everlasting grandeur! everlasting hills! Then, from cañons almost as great, we enter the Bowlder Cañon, cut deep in the metamorphic rocks of foot-hills for seventeen miles, with walls of solid rock that rise precipitously to a height of three thousand feet in many places. A bubbling stream rushes down the centre, broken in its course by clumsy-looking rocks, and the fallen limbs of trees that have been wrenched from the sparse soil and moss in the crevices. The water is discolored and thick. At the head of the cañon is a mining-settlement, and we meet several horsemen traversing a narrow road that clings to the walls—now on one side, and then, leaping the stream, to the other. The pines, that find no haunt too drear, and no soil too sterile, have striven to hide the nakedness of the rocks; but many a branch is withered and decayed, and those still living are dwarfed and sombre. Bowlder City, at the mouth of the cañon, has a population of about fifteen hundred, and is the centre of the most abundant and extensively developed gold, silver, and coal mining districts in the Territory. Within a short distance from it are Central City, Black Hawk, and Georgetown.

James's Peak comes next in our route, and at its foot we see one of the pretty frozen lakes that are scattered all over the range. It is a picturesque and weird yet tenderly sentimental scene. Mr. Moran has caught its spirit admirably, and his picture gives a fair idea of its beauty. The surface is as smooth as a mirror, and reflects the funereal foliage and snowy robes of the slopes as clearly. It is as chaste as morning, and we can think of ice-goblins chasing underneath the folds of virgin snow that the pale moonlight faintly touches and bespangles. The white dress of the mountain hereabout is unchanged the year round, and only yields tribute to the summer heat in thousands of little brooks, that gather together in the greater streams. The lakes themselves are small basins,

CHICAGO LAKE.

not more than two or three acres in extent, and are ice-locked and snow-bound until the summer is far advanced.

You shall not be wearied by a detailed story of our route, or of the routine of our camp. We are on the wing pretty constantly, the photographers and naturalists working with exemplary zeal in adding to their collections. We are never away from the mountains, and never at a spot devoid of beauty. In the morning we climb a hill, and in the evening march down it. Anon we are under the looming shadows of a steep pass or ravine, and then our eyes are refreshed in a green valley—not such a valley as rests at the foot of Alpine hills, but one that has not been transformed by the cultivator—a waste to Eastern eyes, but a paradise, compared with the more rugged forms around, We are not sure that "beauty unadorned is adorned the most" in this instance. A few hedge-rows here and there, a white farm-house on yonder knoll, a level patch of moist, brown earth freshly ploughed, and a leafy, loaded orchard, might change the sentiment of the thing, but would not make it less beautiful.

We encounter civilization, modified by the conditions of frontier life, in the happily-situated little city of Georgetown, which is in a direct line running westward from Denver City, the starting-point of tourist mountaineers. A great many of you have been there, using its hotel as a base of operations in mountaineering. It is locked in a valley surrounded by far-reaching granite hills, with the silver ribbon of Clear Creek flashing its way through, and forests of evergreens soaring to the ridges. A previous traveller has well said that Europe has no place to compare with it. It is five thousand feet higher than the glacier-walled vale of the Chamouni, and even higher than the snow-girt hospice of Saint-Bernard. Roundabout are wonderful "bits" of Nature, and, from the valley itself, we make the ascent of Gray's Peak, the mountain that, of all others in the land, we have heard the most. We toil up a winding road, meeting plenty of company, of a rough sort, on the way. There are many silver-mines in the neighborhood, and we also meet heavily-laden wagons, full of ore, driven by labor-stained men. The air grows clearer and thinner; we leave behind the forests of aspen, and are now among the pines, silver-firs, and spruces. At last we enter a valley, and see afar a majestic peak, which we imagine is our destination. We are wrong. Ours is yet higher, so we ride on, the horses panting and the men restless. The forest still grows thinner; the trees smaller. Below us are the successive valleys through which we have come, and above us the snowy Sierras, tinted with the colors of the sky. Twelve thousand feet above the level of the sea we reach the Stevens silver-mine, the highest point in Colorado where mining is carried on, and then we pass the limit of tree-life, where only dwarfed forms of Alpine or arctic vegetation exist. A flock of white partridges flutter away at our coming, and two or three conies snarl at us from their nests underneath the rocks. Higher yet! Breathless and fatigued, we urge our poor beasts on in the narrow, almost hidden trail, and are rewarded in due time by a safe arrival at our goal.

ERODED SANDSTONES, MONUMENT PARK.

Foremost in the view are the twin peaks, Gray's and Torrey's; but, in a vast area that seems limitless, there are successive rows of pinnacles, some of them entirely wrapped in everlasting snow, others patched with it, some abrupt and pointed, others reaching their climax by soft curves and gradations that are almost imperceptible. We are on the crest of a continent—on the brink of that New World which Agassiz has told us is the Old. The man who could resist the emotion called forth by the scene, is not among our readers, we sincerely hope. There is a sort of enclosure some feet beneath the very summit of Gray's Peak, or, to speak more exactly, a valley surrounded by walls of snow, dotted by occasional bowlders, and sparsely covered with dwarfed vegetation. Here we encamp and light our fires, and smoke our pipes, while our minds are in a trance over the superb reach before us.

Not very many years ago it was a common thing to find a deserted wagon on the plains, with some skeleton men and two skeleton horses not far off. A story is told that, in one case, the tarpaulin was inscribed with the words "Pike's Peak or Bust." Pike's Peak was then an El Dorado to the immigrants, who, in adventurously seeking it, often fell victims on the gore-stained ground of the Sioux Indians. Foremost in the range, it was the most visible from the plains, and was as a star or beacon to the travellers approaching the mountains from the east. Thither we are now bound, destined to call, on the way, at the Chicago Lakes, Monument Park, and the Garden of the Gods. Chicago Lakes lie at the foot of Mount Rosalie, still farther south, and are the source of Chicago Creek. They are high upon the mountain, at the verge of the timber-line, and that shown in Mr. Moran's picture has an elevation of nearly twelve thousand feet above the level of the sea. Mount Rosalie, ridged with snow, and very rugged in appearance, terminates two thousand two hundred feet higher. Another lake, as smooth and lovely as this, and of about the same size, is found near by, and twelve more are scattered, like so many patches of silver, in the vicinity. The water comes from the snow, and is cool and refreshing on the hottest summer days. Trout are abundant in the streams, and allure many travellers over a terribly bad road from Georgetown. Monument Park is probably more familiar to you than other points in our route. It is filled with fantastic groups of eroded sandstone, perhaps the most unique in the Western country, where there are so many evidences of Nature's curious whims. If one should imagine a great number of gigantic sugar-loaves, quite irregular in shape, but all showing the tapering form, varying in height from six feet to nearly fifty, with each loaf capped by a dark, flat stone, not unlike in shape to a college-student's hat, he would have a very clear idea of the columns in Monument Park. They are for the most part ranged along the low hills on each side of the park, which is probably a mile wide, but here and there one stands out in the open plain. On one or two little knolls, apart from the hills, numbers of these columns are grouped, producing the exact effect of cemeteries with their white-marble columns. The stone is very light in color.

PIKE'S PEAK, FROM GARDEN OF THE GODS.

Upper Twin Lake.

Once more we are on our way, and still in the mountains. We linger a while in the Garden of the Gods, which is five miles northwest of Colorado Springs, as you will see by referring to a map, among the magnificent forms that in some places resemble those we have already seen in Monument Park. There are some prominent cliffs, too; but they are not so interesting as others that we have seen, and are simply horizontal strata, thrown by some convulsion into a perpendicular position. At the "gateway" we are between two precipitous walls of sandstone, two hundred feet apart, and three hundred and fifty feet high. Stretching afar is a gently-sloping foot-hill, and, beyond that, in the distance, we have a glimpse of the faint snow-line of Pike's Peak. The scene is strangely impressive. The walls form almost an amphitheatre, enclosing a patch of level earth. In the foreground there is an embankment consisting of apparently detached rocks, some of them distorted into mushroom-shape, and others secreting shallow pools of water in their darkling hollows. The foliage is scarce and deciduous; gloomily pathetic. A rock rises midway between the walls at the gateway, and elsewhere in the garden there are monumental forms that remind us of the valley of the Yellowstone.

Teocalli Mountain.

Pike's Peak, seen from the walls, is about ten miles off. It forms, with its spurs, the southeastern boundary of the South Park. It offers no great difficulties in the ascent, and a good trail for horses has been made to the summit, where an "Old Probabilities" has stationed an officer to forecast the coming storms.

Now we bear away to Fairplay, where we join the principal division of the expedition, and thence we visit together Mount Lincoln, Western Pass, the Twin Lakes, and other points in the valley of the Arkansas; cross the National or Mother range into the Elk Mountains; proceed up the Arkansas and beyond its head-waters to the Mount of the Holy Cross. We are exhausting our space, not our subject, and we can only describe at length a few spots in the magnificent country included in our itinerary. At the beginning we spoke about Mount Lincoln, and the glorious view obtained from its summit. When named, during the war, this peak was thought to be eighteen thousand feet high, but more recent measurements have brought it down to about fourteen thousand feet—lower, in fact, than Pike's, Gray's, Long's, Yale, or Harvard, the highest of which has yet to be determined. But its summit commands points in a region of country nearly twenty-five thousand square miles in extent, embracing the grandest natural beauties, a bewildering reach of peaks, valleys, cañons, rivers, and lakes. We find, too, on Mount Lincoln, some lovely Alpine flowers, which grow in profusion even on the very summit, and are of nearly every color and great fragrance. Professor J. D. Whitney, who accompanied the expedition, picked several sweetly-smelling bunches of delicate blue-bells within five feet of the dome of Mount Lincoln. These tender little plants are chilled every night to freezing, and draw all their nourishment from the freshly-melted snow.

Heretofore we have spoken complainingly, it may seem, of the sombre quality of all we have seen, and its deficient power of evoking human sympathy. But at the Twin Lakes we have no more occasion for morbid brooding, but a chance to go into healthy raptures, and to admire some tender, almost pastural scenery. The course of the Arkansas River is southward hereabout, touching the base of the central chain of the mountains. So it continues for one hundred miles, then branching eastward toward the Mississippi. In the lower part of the southward course the valley expands, and is bordered on the east by an irregular mass of low, broken hill-ranges, and on the west by the central range. Twenty miles above this point the banks are closely confined, and form a very picturesque gorge; still further above they again expand, and here are nestled the beautiful Twin Lakes. The larger is about two and a half miles long and a mile and a half wide; the smaller about half that size. At the upper end they are girt by steep and rugged heights; below they are bounded by undulating hills of gravel and bowlders. A broad stream connects the two, and then hurries down the plain to join and swell the Arkansas. Our illustration does not exaggerate the chaste beauty of the upper lake, the smaller of the two. The contour of the surrounding hills is marvellously varied: here softly curving, and yonder soaring to an abrupt peak. In some things it transports us to the western Highlands of Scotland, and, as with their waters, its depths are swarming with the most delicately flavored, the most spirited and largest trout. Sportsmen come here in considerable numbers; and not the least charming object to be met on the banks is an absorbed, contemplative man, seated on some glacier-thrown bowlder, with his slender rod poised and bending gracefully, and a pretty wicker basket, half hidden in the moist grass at his side, ready for the gleaming fish that flaunts his gorgeous colors in the steadily-lapping waters.

We advance from the Twin Lakes into the very heart of the Rocky Mountains, and sojourn in a quiet little valley while the working-force of the expedition explores the

SNOW-MASS MOUNTAIN.

neighboring country. Two summits are ascended from our station, one of them a round peak of granite, full fourteen thousand feet above the level of the sea, and only to

Elk-Lake Cascade.

be reached by assiduous and tiresome scrambling over fractured rocks. This we name La Plata. We are on the grandest uplift on the continent, Professor Whitney believes. The range is of unswerving direction, running north and south for nearly a hundred miles, and is broken into countless peaks over twelve thousand feet high. It is penetrated by deep ravines, which formerly sent great glaciers into the valley; it is composed of granite and eruptive rocks. The northernmost point is the Mount of the Holy Cross, and that we shall visit soon. Advancing again through magnificent upland meadows and amphitheatres, we come at last to Red-Mountain Pass, so named from a curious line of light near the summit, marked for half a mile with a brilliant crimson stain, verging into yellow from the oxidation of iron in the volcanic material. The effect of this, as may be imagined, is wonderfully beautiful. Thence we traverse several ravines in the shadow of the imposing granite mountains, enter fresh valleys, and contemplate fresh wonders. The ardent geologists of the expedition, ever alert, discover one day a ledge of limestone containing corals, and soon we are in a region filled with enormous and surprising developments of that material. We pitch our tents near the base of an immense pyramid, capped with layers of red sandstone, which we name Teocalli, from the Aztec word, meaning " pyramid of sacrifice." The view from our camp is — we

MOUNTAIN OF THE HOLY CROSS.

should say surpassing, could we remember or decide which of all the beauties we have is the grandest. Two hills incline toward the valley where we are stationed, ultimately falling into each other's arms. Between their shoulders there is a broad gap, and, in the rear, the majestic form of the Teocalli reaches to heaven.

In the distance we have seen two mountains which are temporarily called Snow-Mass and Black Pyramid. The first of these we are now ascending. It is a terribly hard road to travel. The slopes consist of masses of immense granitic fragments, the rock-bed from which they came appearing only occasionally. When we reach the crest, we find it also broken and cleft in masses and pillars. Professor Whitney ingeniously reckons that an industrious man, with a crow-bar, could, by a week's industrious exertion, reduce the height of the mountain one or two hundred feet. Some of the members of the expedition amuse themselves by the experiment, toppling over great fragments, which thunder down the slopes, and furrow the wide snow-fields below. It is this snow-field which forms the characteristic feature of the mountain as seen in the distance. There is about a square mile of unbroken white, and, lower down still, a lake of blue water. A little to the northward of Snow-Mass, the range rises into another yet greater mountain. The two are known to miners as "The Twins," although they are not at all alike, as the provisional names we bestowed upon them indicate. After mature deliberation the expedition rechristen them the White House and the Capitol, under which names we suppose they will be familiar to future generations. Not a great distance from here, leading down the mountain from · Elk Lake, is a picturesque cascade, that finds its way through deep gorges and cañons to the Rio Grande.

The Mountain of the Holy Cross is next reached. This is the most celebrated mountain in the region, but its height, which has been over-estimated, is not more than fourteen thousand feet. The ascent is exceedingly toilsome even for inured mountaineers, and I might give you an interesting chapter describing the difficulties that beset us. There is a very beautiful peculiarity in the mountain, as its name shows. The principal peak is composed of gneiss, and the cross fractures of the rock on the eastern slope have made two great fissures, which cut into one another at right angles, and hold their snow in the form of a cross the summer long.

CHAPTER THREE

The Cañons of the Colorado
from the northern Rockies to the Grand Canyon

Canyon country: redrock fantasies carved into the earth, raging rivers in bone dry land. Even today — jaded as we are by travel and images of travel — the gorges and canyons of the Colorado river strike us as the most surrealistic landscapes on our continent. But the rare 19th century travelers who saw them, timidly straggling into this dreamlike canyon country in the wake of Powell's explorations, timidly peering over the edges of these great chromatic wounds in the desert, were simply reduced to stunned silence. Their notoriously lavish prose proved unequal to the task, their extravagant adjectives and arching metaphors simply collapsed under the weight of so much beauty, such other-worldly strangeness. And they took rhetorical refuge from the mystery and grandeur of these southwestern canyonlands in simple statistics.

At least that's my reading of the reactions of travelers like J. E. Colburn, the author of this chapter. What modern writer would take such pains to explain that Marble Canyon is "sixty-five and a half miles long" while the longer Grand Canyon is "two hundred seventeen and a half miles long." And that its walls tower up to "six thousand two hundred and thirty-three feet." This is not the grand and grandiose prose that we've grown used to in early descriptions of the west. It is more the cautious report of someone who has just had a peek inside a real-life treasure trove, and comes back thinking no one will believe him.

The illustrations of this chapter, however, take the opposite tack altogether. They are mostly penned from early photographs, not from personal observation as were most of Thomas Moran's western landscapes; and they take us into a deep and mysterious world, the wilderness setting for a gothic romance. Without color to capture the purple-red-ochre spectrum of these canyons, Moran concentrated on shadows and created a canyon-bottom decor in shades of black. A wonderful contrast with the other chapters of this book where his images, artful as they are, seem closer to the documentary reality of the mountain West than the fevered prose that they illustrate.

L.T-F.

THE CAÑONS OF THE COLORADO.

WITH ILLUSTRATIONS BY THOMAS MORAN.

Bonita Bend.

NONE of the works of Nature on the American Continent, where many things are done by her upon a scale of grandeur elsewhere unknown, approach in magnificence and wonder the cañons of the Colorado. The river-system of the Colorado is, in extent of area drained, the second or third in the United States. The drainage of the Mississippi is, of course, far more extensive, and the drainage of the Columbia is nearly equal, or perhaps a little greater. It is characteristic of the Colorado that nearly all the streams which unite to form it, or which flow into it, are confined in deep and narrow gorges, with walls often perpendicular. Sometimes the walls rise directly from the water's edge, so that there is only room between for the passage of the stream. In other places, the bottoms of the gorges widen out into valleys, through which roads may pass ; and sometimes they contain small tracts of arable land. For the most part, the walls of the cañons of the Colorado-River system are not above a few hundred feet in height ; and yet, there are more than a thousand miles of cañons where they rise ten or twelve hundred feet in perpendicular cliffs. The Grand Cañon, which Major Powell calls " the most profound chasm known on the globe," is, for a distance of over two hundred miles, at no point less than four thousand feet deep.

The Green River, which is familiar to every person who has passed over the Union Pacific Railroad, is one of the principal sources of the Colorado. The first successful attempt to explore the Grand Cañon was made by Major J. W. Powell, in 1869. He reached it then by descending the Green River with boats, built in Chicago, and carried by rail to Green-River Station. He accomplished the voyage of nearly a thousand miles in three months, one month being occupied in the passage of the Grand Cañon. Father Escalante had seen the Colorado in 1776, and the màp which he constructed shows clearly the point at which he crossed. Fremont and Whipple had seen the cañon ; and

Ives, in his expedition of 1857 and 1858, saw the Kanab, one of its largest branches, which he mistook for the Grand Cañon itself. But, previous to Major Powell's voyage of exploration, the course of a great part of the river was as little known as the sources of the Nile; and the accounts of the wonders of the Grand Cañon were held by many to be rather mythical, and greatly exaggerated.

The Colorado is formed by the junction of the Grand and Green Rivers in the eastern part of Utah. The distance from Green-River Station, by the course of the river, to the junction of the two streams, is four hundred fifty-eight and a half miles. The cañons begin very soon after leaving the railroad, and in the series named are Flaming Gorge, Kingfisher, and Red Cañons, Cañon of Lodore, Whirlpool and Yampa Cañons, Cañon of Desolation, Gray, Labyrinth, Stillwater, Cataract, Narrow, Glen, and Marble Cañons. Each has some peculiar characteristic, which, in most instances, is indicated by the name. There is generally no break in the walls between the different cañons, the divisions being marked by remarkable changes in their geological structure. The cañons whose names above precede Cataract, are on Green River before it joins the waters of the Grand.

Labyrinth is one of the lower cañons of the Green River. It is a wide and beautiful cañon, with comparatively low walls, but perpendicular and impassable. Indeed, from Gunnison's Crossing, one hundred and sixteen miles above the junction of the Grand and Green, to the running out of the Grand Cañon, a distance of five hundred eighty-seven and a half miles, there are only two places, and they are not more than a mile apart, where the river and its chasm can be crossed. At one point in Labyrinth Cañon, the river makes a long bend, in the bow of which it sweeps around a huge circular *butte*, whose regular and perpendicular walls look as though they might have been laid by a race of giant craftsmen. At a distance the pile resembles a vast, turret-shaped fortress, deserted and partly broken down. This point in the river is called Bonita Bend, and a view of it has been drawn by Mr. Moran from photographs taken by Major Powell's party. The waters in this cañon are smooth and shoal, and afforded the explorers, for many miles, a grateful rest from the toil and danger of shooting rapids, or making wearisome portages of the boats.

The junction of the Grand and Green Rivers brings together a flood of waters about equal in volume to the flow of Niagara. The Grand and Green meet in a narrow gorge more than two thousand feet deep; and at this point the cañons of the Colorado begin.

The first is called Cataract Cañon. It is about forty miles long. The descent of the river through this cañon is very great, and the velocity acquired by the current is sometimes equal to the speed of the fastest railroad-train. Great buttresses of the walls stand out into the rushing flood at frequent intervals, turning the rapid current into boiling whirlpools, which were encountered by the adventurous boatmen with great peril and

GLEN CAÑON.

labor. At the foot of Cataract Cañon, the walls of the chasm approach each other, and, for a distance of seven miles, the water rushes through Narrow Cañon at the rate of forty miles an hour.

At the end of Narrow Cañon, the character of the gorge changes, and, from that point to the place where the Paria River enters the Colorado, a distance of a hundred and forty and a half miles, it is called Glen Cañon. At the mouth of the Paria, a trail leads down the cliffs to the bottom of the cañon on both sides, and animals and wagons can be taken down and crossed over in boats. The Indians swim across on logs.

A mile above the Paria is the Crossing of the Fathers, where Father Escalante and his hundred priests passed across the cañon. An alcove in this cañon, which the artist has drawn, illustrates the general character of the walls, and the scenery from which the cañon takes its name. The smooth and precipitous character of the walls of Glen Cañon is well shown in the illustration. The chasm is carved in homogeneous red sandstone, and in some places, for a thousand feet on the face of the rock, there is scarce a check or seam.

Buttresses of Marble Cañon.

The most beautiful of all the cañons begins at the mouth of the Paria, and extends to the junction of the Little Colorado, or Chiquito, as it is called by the Indians. This part of the gorge is named Marble Cañon, and is sixty-five and a half miles long. The walls are of limestone or marble, beautifully carved and polished, and the forms assumed have the most remarkable resemblances to ruined architecture. The colors of the marble are various— pink, brown, gray, white, slate-color, and vermilion. The beautiful forms, with a suggestion of the grand scale on which they are constructed, are given by the two views in this cañon, which the artist has drawn. But it is only on large canvas, and by the use of the many-tinted brush, that any reproduction can be made, approaching truthfulness, of the combination of the grand and beautiful exhibited in the sculpturing, the colors, and the awful depth, of Marble Cañon.

MARBLE CAÑON.

The Marble Cañon runs out at the junction of the Chiquito and Colorado, at which point the Grand Cañon begins. The head of the Grand Cañon is in the northeastern part of Arizona, and it runs out in the northwestern part, lying wholly within that Territory. Its general course is westerly, but it makes two great bends to the south. It is two hundred and seventeen and a half miles long, and the walls vary in height from four thousand to six thousand two hundred and thirty-three feet. It is cut through a series of levels of varying altitudes, the chasm being deepest, of course, where it passes through the highest. There are in the cañon no perpendicular cliffs more than three thousand feet in height. At that elevation from the river, the sides slope back, and rise by a series of perpendicular cliffs and benches to the level of the surrounding country. In many places it is possible to find gorges or side-cañons, cutting down through the upper cliffs, by which it is possible, and in some instances easy, to approach to the edge of the wall which rises perpendicularly from the river. At three thousand feet above the river, the chasm is often but a few hundred feet wide. At the highest elevation mentioned, the distance across is generally from five to ten miles.

At various places the chasm is cleft through the primal granite rock to the depth of twenty-eight hundred feet. In those parts of the cañon, which are many miles of its whole extent, the chasm is narrow, the walls rugged, broken, and precipitous, and the navigation of the river dangerous. The daring voyagers gave profound thanks, as though they had escaped from death, whenever they passed out from between the walls of granite into waters confined by lime or sandstone. Mr. Moran has drawn a section of these granite walls, showing some of the pinnacles and buttresses which are met at every turn of the river. The waters rush through the granite cañons at terrific speed. Great waves, formed by the irregular sides and bottom, threatened every moment to engulf the boats. Spray dashes upon the rocks fifty feet above the edge of the river, and the gorge is filled with a roar as of thunder, which is heard many miles away.

Fortunately, the wonders of the Grand Cañon can now be seen without incurring any of the peril, and but little of the hardship, endured by Major Powell and his companions. The writer of this, and Mr. Moran, the artist, visited two of the most interesting points in the cañon in July and August, 1873. We travelled by stage in hired vehicles—they could not be called carriages—and on horseback from Salt-Lake City to Toquerville, in Southwestern Utah, and thence about sixty miles to Kanab, just north of the Arizona line. Quite passable roads have been constructed by the Mormons this whole distance of about four hundred miles. At Kanab we met Professor A. H. Thompson, in charge of the topographical work of Major Powell's survey, and, with guides and companions from his camp, we visited the cañon.

Our first journey was to the Toroweap Valley, about seventy miles. By following down this valley we passed through the upper line of cliffs to the edge of a chasm cut

WALLS OF THE GRAND CAÑON.

in red sandstone and vermilion-colored limestone, or marble, twenty-eight hundred feet deep, and about one thousand feet wide. Creeping out carefully on the edge of the precipice, we could look down directly upon the river, fifteen times as far away as the waters of the Niagara are below the bridge. Mr. Hillers, who has passed through the cañon with Major Powell, was with us, and he informed us that the river below was a raging torrent; and yet it looked, from the top of the cliff, like a small, smooth, and sluggish river. The view looking up the cañon is magnificent and beautiful beyond the most extravagant conception of the imagination. In the foreground lies the profound gorge, with a mile or two of the river seen in its deep bed. The eye looks twenty miles or more through what appears like a narrow valley, formed by the upper line of cliffs. The many-colored rocks in which this valley is carved, project into it in vast headlands, two thousand feet high, wrought into beautiful but gigantic architectural forms. Within an hour of the time of sunset the effect is strangely awful, weird, and dazzling. Every moment until light is gone the scene shifts, as one monumental pile passes into shade, and another, before unobserved, into light. But no power of description can aid the imagination to picture it, and only the most gifted artist, with all the materials that artists can command, is able to suggest any thing like it.

Our next visit was to the Kai-bal Plateau, the highest plateau through which the cañon cuts. It was only after much hard labor, and possibly a little danger, that we reached a point where we could see the river, which we did from the edge of Powell Plateau, a small plain severed from the main-land by a precipitous gorge, two thousand feet deep, across which we succeeded in making a passage. Here we beheld one of the most awful scenes upon our globe. While upon the highest point of the plateau, a terrific thunder-storm burst over the cañon. The lighting flashed from crag to crag. A thousand streams gathered on the surrounding plains, and dashed down into the depths of the cañon in water-falls many times the height of Niagara. The vast chasm which we saw before us, stretching away forty miles in one direction and twenty miles in another, was nearly seven thousand feet deep. Into it all the domes of the Yosemite, if plucked up from the level of that valley, might be cast, together with all the mass of the White Mountains in New Hampshire, and still the chasm would not be filled.

Kanab Cañon is about sixty miles long, and, by following its bed, one can descend to the bottom of the Grand Cañon. It is a very difficult task, requiring several days' severe labor. We were forced, by lack of time, which other engagements absorbed, to abandon the undertaking The picture drawn by the artist of a pinnacle in one of the angles of the Kanab is from a photograph taken by Mr. Hillers. The pinnacle itself is about eight hundred, and the wall in the background of the illustration more than four thousand feet in altitude. A railroad is projected from Salt-Lake City to the southern settlements, and, when it is constructed, some of the most remarkable portions of the Grand Cañon of the Colorado will be as accessible as the valley of the Yosemite.

KANAB CAÑON.

CHAPTER FOUR

The Plains and the Sierras
By train across the Rockies, & on to the Pacific

Riding a train across the country is not, admittedly, everyone's idea of an adventure. But it seems much more adventurous if we put ourselves in the place of travelers making this journey to the Pacific only a few years after the golden spike was driven, and long, long before such journeys became commonplace.

"The Plains to the Sierra" is the narrative of such a multi-day train trip across two great ranges, the Rockies and the Sierra, and the intervening basin-and-range country that the author tends to dismiss as unrelieved badlands — which he genteelly refers to as "terres mauvaises." In a way, this journey was a mountain adventure without many mountains. The railroad builders cunningly staged an end-run around the main upthrust of the Rockies — crossing the range in southern Wyoming, just south of the Wind River peaks; steaming gently uphill for hours over scarcely tilted plains, to a continental divide that only seemed an invisible swell in a wide landscape. Far more dramatic for the passenger, the Truckee-Tahoe-Donner Pass route across California's High Sierra was also a way of avoiding the wilder Sierra crest further south.

This chapter paints a reasonably faithful panorama of what the early traveler saw out the window of his Pullman, but the author, E. L. Burlingame, was too much a child of his time to restrict himself to simple facts. Blithely ignorant of the reality of the Mormons hard-won conquest of western Utah, he presents them as "deluded" heathens, abandoning common sense and rich Eastern farmlands to waste their energies farming a desert.... And since the new railroad skirted most of the truly spectacular mountain terrain between Omaha and Oakland, our guide simply fills it in with rhetorical flights — and even better, with extensive quotations from Clarence King, the pioneer mountaineer and explorer of the Sierra Nevada.

At one point in his journey, our author speaks naively of a landscape "that cities and settlements cannot destroy." But this chapter's final images of the train rushing in under the "great green oaks of Oakland" show anyone familiar with the Bay Area today just how wrong he was. The great green oaks of Oakland are long gone.

L.T-F.

THE PLAINS AND THE SIERRAS.

WITH ILLUSTRATIONS BY THOMAS MORAN.

Witches' Rocks, Weber Cañon.

THE present banishes the past so quickly in this busy continent that to the
younger generation of to-day it already seems a very dreamy and distant heroic
age when men went out upon the great prairies of the West as upon a dreaded kind

of unknown sea. Even now, perhaps, there is a little spice of adventure for the quieter New-England citizen, as he gathers around him the prospective contents of a comfortable travelling-trunk, and glances at his long slip of printed railway-tickets, preparatory to thundering westward to look out at the great stretch of the Plains from the ample window of a perfectly-upholstered sleeping-car; but how remote the day seems when men tightened their pistol-belts and looked to their horses, and throbbed (if they were young) with something of the proud consciousness of explorers; and so set out, from the frontier settlement of civilization, upon that great ocean of far-reaching, level grass-land and desert, to cross which was a deed to be talked of like the voyage of the old Minyæ! A single title of Mr. Harte's has preserved for us the whole spirit of those seemingly old-time journeys; he has called the travellers "the Argonauts of '49," and in this one phrase lies the complete picture of that already dim and distant venture—the dreaded crossing of "the Plains."

But, although the "prairie schooner"—the great white-tented wagon of the gold-seekers and the pioneers—and its adjuncts, and the men that rode beside it, have disappeared, we cannot change the Plains themselves in a decade. We encroach a little upon their borders, it may be, and learn of a narrow strip of their surface, but they themselves remain practically untouched by the civilization that brushes over them; they close behind the scudding train like the scarce broader ocean behind the stoutest steamer of the moderns—a vast expanse as silent and unbroken and undisturbed as it lay centuries before ever rail or keel was dreamed of. It is our point of view that has changed, not they; and for all of us there remain the same wonders to be looked upon in this great half-known region as were there for the earliest Indian fighter—the first of the adventurous souls that went mine-hunting toward the Golden Gate.

Our time, it is true, attaches a different signification to the title, "the Plains," from that which it bore little more than a quarter of a century ago. In reality, there extends from the very central portion of the now well-peopled Western States to the very foot of the Rocky Mountains one vast reach of prairie—the most remarkable, in all its features, on the globe. On the eastern portion of this are now the thoroughly settled, grain-bearing States—full of fertile farms and great cities, and no longer connected in our minds, as they were in those of men a generation before us, with the untried lands of exploration and adventure. For us, the boundary of the region of the comparatively unknown has been driven back beyond the Mississippi, beyond the Missouri, even; and the Eastern citizen, be he ever so thoroughly the town-bred man, is at home until he crosses the muddy, sluggish water that flows under Council Bluffs, and hardly passes out of the land of most familiar objects until the whistle of the " Pacific express," that carries him, is no longer heard in Omaha, and he is fairly under way on the great level of Nebraska.

The route of the Pacific Railway is not only that which for many years will be the most familiar path across the Plains, and not only that which passes nearest to the well-known emigrant-road of former days, but it is also the road which, though it misses the nobler beauties of the Rocky Mountains, shows the traveller the prairie itself

Red Buttes, Laramie Plains.

in perhaps as true and characteristic an aspect as could be found on any less-tried course. It passes through almost every change of prairie scenery —the fertile land of the east and the alkali region farther on; past the historic outposts of the old pioneers; among low *buttes* and infrequent "islands;" and over a country abounding in points of view from which one may take in all the features that mark this portion of the continent. To the south, the great level expanse is hardly interrupted before the shore of the Gulf of Mexico is reached, and the Mexican boundary; to the north, the hills and high table-land of the Upper Missouri are the only breaks this side of the Canadian border. Through almost the middle of this vast and clear expanse the Union Pacific Railway runs east and west—a line of life flowing like a river through the great plain—the Kansas Pacific joining it at the middle of its course, a tributary of no small importance.

Omaha—most truly typical of those border towns that, all the world over, spring up on the verge of the civilized where the unexplored begins—stands looking out upon the muddy water of the Missouri, and watching with interested eyes that transient traveller whom it generally entices in vain to linger long within its precincts—a town that has been all its life a starting-place; to which hardly anybody has ever come with the thought of staying, so far as one can learn from hearsay; and yet, in spite of the fact

DIAL ROCK, RED BUTTES, LARAMIE PLAINS.

that every man seems to arrive only with the thought of departing, a prosperous, thrifty town, not without a look of permanence, though not of any age beyond the memory of the youngest inhabitant. In its directory, which the writer once chanced to read with some care, in a waiting hour, you may find facts that will startle you about the rapidity of its growth and the splendor of its resources. At its station, one feels a little of the old-time pioneer feeling, as he seems to cut the chain that binds him to Eastern life, and is whirled out upon the great grassy sea he has looked at wonderingly from the Omaha hills.

The word "valley," in this apparently unbroken plain, seems a misnomer; but it is everywhere used—as in regions where its significance is truer—for the slight depression that accompanies the course of every stream; and an old traveller of the Plains will tell you that you are "entering the valley of the Platte," or "coming out of the Papillon Valley," with as much calmness as though you were entering or leaving the rockiest and wildest cañon of the Sierras. And the valley of the Platte, whereof he speaks, lies before one almost immediately after he has left the Missouri behind him. There is only a short reach of railway to the northwest, a sharp turn to the westward, and the clear stream of the river is beside the track—a clear, full channel if the water is high, a collection of brooks threading their way through sandy banks if it is low. For more than a whole day the railway runs beside the stream, and neither to the north nor south is there noteworthy change in the general features of the scenery. A vast, fertile plain, at first interrupted here and there by bluffs, and for some distance not seldom dotted by a settler's house, or by herds of cattle; then a more monotonous region, still green and bright in aspect; farther on—beyond Fort Kearney, and Plum Creek, and McPherson, all memorable stations with many associations from earlier times—a somewhat sudden dying away of the verdure, and a barren country, broken by a few ravines. This, again, gives place, however, to a better region as the Wyoming boundary is approached.

Along this reach of the railway, in its earlier days, stood ambitious "cities," two or three whose ruins are the only reminders now of their existence. They are odd features of this part of the great prairie, these desolate remains of places not a little famous in their time, and now almost forgotten. The walls of deserted *adobe* houses, wherein men sat and planned great futures for these towns in embryo, look at you drearily, not seldom watching over the graves of their owners, whose schemings were nipped in the very bud by the decisive revolver-bullet or the incisive bowie, as the unquiet denizens of the mushroom metropolis extirpated their fellow-citizens like true pioneers, and "moved on" to the next "terminus of the road."

The Wyoming border crossed, a new region is entered. The Plains do not end, but they are already closely bordered, within sight, by the far-outlying spurs of the Rocky Mountains. Beyond the civilized oasis of Cheyenne, the scenery takes on a darker look, and, if one chances to come to the little station of Medicine Bow when

Buttes, Green River.

the sunset begins to cast long shadows from the black mountains on the southern side of the North Fork of the Platte, there is something almost sombre in the aspect of the shaded plain. The Laramie plains have just been passed; indeed, they still lie to the northward. Hills break the monotony of their horizon, and here and there the regular forms of castellated *buttes* stand out sharply against the sky. The far-off Red Buttes are most noteworthy and most picturesque of these;

73

grouped together like giant fortresses, with fantastic towers and walls, they lift ragged edges above the prairie, looking lonely, weird, and strong. Among the singular shapes their masses of stone assume, the strangely-formed and pillar-like Dial Rocks tower up— four columns of worn and scarred sandstone, like the supports of some ruined cromlech built by giants. About them, and, indeed, through the whole region about the little settlements and army-posts, from the place called Wyoming, on to Bitter Creek—ominously named—the country is a barren, unproductive waste. The curse of the sage-brush, and even of alkali, is upon it, and it is dreary and gloomy everywhere save on the hills.

Only with the approach to Green River does the verdure come again—and then only here and there, generally close by the river-bank. Here the picturesque forms of the buttes reappear—a welcome relief to the monotony that has marked the outlook during the miles of level desert that are past. The distance, too, is changed, and no longer is like the great surface of a sea. To the north, forming the horizon, stretches the Wind-River Range—named with a breezy poetry that we miss in the later nomenclature of the race that has followed after the pioneers. To the south lie the Uintah Mountains.

At some little distance from the railway the great Black Buttes rise up for hundreds of feet, terminating in round and rough-ribbed towers. And other detached columns of stone stand near them—the Pilot, seen far off in the view that Mr. Moran has drawn of the river and its cliffs. And through all this region fantastic forms abound everywhere, the architecture of Nature exhibited in sport. An Eastern journalist—a traveller here in the first days of the Pacific Railway—has best enumerated the varied shapes. All about one, he says, lie "long, wide troughs, as of departed rivers; long, level embankments, as of railroad-tracks or endless fortifications; huge, quaint hills, suddenly rising from the plain, bearing fantastic shapes; great square mounds of rock and earth, half-formed, half-broken pyramids—it would seem as if a generation of giants had built and buried here, and left their work to awe and humble a puny succession."

The Church Butte is the grandest of the groups that rise in this singular and striking series of tower-like piles of stone. It lies somewhat further on, beyond the little station of Bryan, and forms a compact and imposing mass of rock, with an outlying spur that has even more than the main body the air of human, though gigantic architecture. It "imposes on the imagination," says Mr. Bowles, in one of his passages of clear description, "like a grand old cathedral going into decay—quaint in its crumbling ornaments, majestic in its height and breadth." And of the towering forms of the whole group, he says: "They seem, like the more numerous and fantastic illustrations of Nature's frolicsome art in Southern Colorado, to be the remains of granite hills that wind and water, and especially the sand whirlpools that march with lordly force through the air—literally moving mountains—have left to tell the story of their own achievements. Not unfitly, there as here, they have won the title of 'Monuments to the Gods.'"

CLIFFS OF GREEN RIVER.

This point on the Plains, where the mountains—the main chains running northwest and southeast—seem to send out transverse ranges and outlying spurs to intersect the prairie in all directions—if, indeed, we may speak of prairie any longer where the level reaches are so small as here among the Rocks—has interests beyond those of its merely picturesque scenery. While we have spoken of the cliffs and *buttes*, the route we are pursuing has crossed the "backbone of the continent"—that great water-shed where the waters that flow through the whole east of the country separate from those that descend toward the west. It is at Sherman—which its proud neighbors and few residents will haughtily but truly describe to you as "the highest railway-station in the world"—

Church Butte, Utah.

that the greatest elevation is reached; for the little group of buildings there lies eight thousand two hundred and thirty-five feet above sea-level. It is impossible to realize that this height has been attained, the ascent has been so gradual, the scenery so un-marked by those sharp and steep forms which we are accustomed always to associate with great mountains.

It is a characteristic of this whole portion of the Rocky-Mountain chain, and one that disappoints many a traveller, that there are here no imposing and ragged peaks, no sharp summits, no snow-covered passes, and little that is wild and rugged. All that those who remember Switzerland have been accustomed to connect in their minds with great

Castle Rock, Echo Cañon.

groups of mountain-masses must be sought elsewhere. The Plains themselves rise; one does not leave them in order to climb. Over a vast, grass-covered, almost unbroken, gradual slope, extending over hundreds of miles of country, the wayfarer has come imperceptibly to the great water-shed. It is scenery of prairie, not of hills and peaks, that has surrounded his journey.

For the last fifty miles, indeed, before the arrival at Sherman, the rise has been barely appreciable; but that is all. A new circumstance makes the descent from the great height much more perceptible and enjoyable through a new sensation. It is then that the traveller over duller Eastern roads, who has flattered himself that the "lightning express" of his own region was the highest possible form of railway speed, first learns the real meaning of a "down grade." The descent from Sherman to the Laramie Plains is a new experience to such people as have not slid down a Russian ice-hill, or fallen from a fourth-story window. Let the hardy individual who would enjoy it to the full betake himself to the last platform of the last car, or the foremost platform of the front one, and there hold hard to brake or railing, to watch the bewitched world spin and whirl.

But we have returned a long distance on our course. We have reached the Church Butte, beyond Bryan, and had crossed Green River, near the place where, on the old overland stage-route and the emigrant-road, travellers used years ago to ford the stream—no unwelcome task, with that great Bitter-Creek waste of alkali still fresh in the memories and hardly out of their view. At Bryan Station, too, there is an offshoot from the regular path, in the form of a long stage-road, leading away into the northeast to the picturesque mining-region of Sweetwater, a hundred miles distant, where man has spent endless toil in searching for deceptive " leads."

The main line of the great railway goes on beyond Green River through the valley of a stream that flows down from the Uintah Mountains; and, leaving at the south Fort Bridger and crossing the old Mormon road, enters Utah. A little farther, and we are among the noblest scenes of the journey this side the far-away Sierras.

As on the Rhine, the long stretch of the river from Mainz to Cologne has been for years, by acknowledgment, "*the* river," so that portion of the Pacific Railway that lies between Wasatch and Ogden, in this northernmost corner of Utah, will some day be that part of the journey across the centre of the continent that will be especially regarded by the tourist as necessary to be seen beyond all others. It does not in grandeur approach the mountain-scenery near the western coast, but it is unique; it is something, the counterpart of which you can see nowhere in the world; and, long after the whole Pacific journey is as hackneyed in the eyes of Europeans and Americans as is the Rhine tour now, this part of it will keep its freshness among the most marked scenes of the journey. It is a place which cities and settlements cannot destroy.

A short distance west from Wasatch Station the road passes through a tunnel nearly eight hundred feet in length. The preparation for what is to come could not be better; and, indeed, the whole bleak and dreary region that has been passed over adds so much to the freshness and picturesqueness of these Utah scenes that it may very possibly have contributed not a little to the enthusiasm they have called forth. From the darkness the train emerges suddenly, and, tunnel and cutting being passed, there lies before the traveller a view of the green valley before the entrance to Echo Cañon. Through it flows the Weber River, bordered with trees, and making a scene that is suddenly deprived of all the weirdness and look of dreary devastation that has marked the country through so many miles of this long journey. The valley is not so broad, so pastoral in aspect, as that which comes after the wild scenery of the first cañon is passed; but it is like a woodland valley of home lying here in the wilderness.

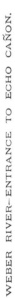

WEBER RIVER—ENTRANCE TO ECHO CAÑON.

Near the head of Echo Cañon stands Castle Rock, one of the noblest of the great natural landmarks that are passed in all the route—a vast and ragged pile of massive stone, fantastically cut, by all those mighty forces that toil through the centuries, into the very semblance of a mountain-fortress. A cavernous opening simulates a giant door of entrance between its rounded and overhanging towers; the jagged points above are like the ruins of battlements left bristling and torn after combats of Titans; the huge layers of its worn sides seem to have been builded by skilful hands; and the great rounded foundations, from which the sandy soil has been swept away, would appear rooted in the very central earth. It surmounts a lofty, steep-sided eminence, and frowns down with an awesome strength and quiet on the lonely valley below it.

It is a great ruin of Nature, not of human structure; and its grandeur is different in kind and in degree from those other relics in an older world, wherewith human history is associated in every mind, which hold for us everywhere the memories of human toil and action. It is a strangely different feeling that this grand pile, made with no man's hands, gives us as we look up at it. It has stood alone longer than whole races have been in the world. Its lines were shaped with no thought, it seems, of those that were to see them; the purposeless wind and sand and rain have been busy at it for vast cycles of time, and at the end it is a thing of art—a great lesson of rude architecture.

Beyond it the road enters the Echo Cañon itself. It is a narrow gorge between rocky walls that tower hundreds of feet above its uneven floor, along which the river runs with a stream as bright and clear as at its very source. Not simply a straight cut between its precipices of red-and-dark-stained stone, but a winding valley, with every turn presenting some new variation of its wonderful scenery. On the mountains that form its sides there is little verdure—only a dwarfed growth of pine scattered here and there, leaving the steeper portions of the rock bare and ragged in outline. Now and then there are little openings, where the great walls spread apart and little glades are formed; but these are no less picturesque than the wilder passages.

There are memorable places here. Half-way down the gorge is Hanging Rock, where Brigham Young spoke to his deluded hundreds after their long pilgrimage, and pointed out to them that they approached their Canaan—preached the Mormons' first sermon in the " Promised Land." Full of all that is wild and strange, as is this rocky valley, seen even from the prosaic window of a whirling railway-car, what must it have been with the multitude of fanatics, stranger than all its strangeness, standing on its varied floor and looking up at the speaking prophet, whom they half believed, half feared? The weary multitude of half-excited, half-stolid faces turned toward the preacher; the coarse, strong, wild words of the leader echoing from the long-silent rocks—why has no one ever pictured for us all of the scene that could be pictured?

A relic of the early Mormon days, but not a proud one, is some miles away from

MONUMENT ROCK, ECHO CAÑON.

this, high on the rocks; an unnoticeable ruin of the little fortifications once for a very short time occupied by the United States troops, in the presidency of Buchanan, when a trifling detachment of soldiers made a perfectly vain and indecisive show of interfering with the rule of the rebellious saints. The ruin is hardly more important than the attempt; yet it deserves mention, if only as commemorative of an episode that the future historian, if he notes it at all, will connect with this rocky region of hard marches and ill-fated emigrants.

The cañon is not long; the train dashes through it at sharp pace; and suddenly, without passing any point of view that gives the traveller a warning glance ahead, it turns and dashes out into the beautiful and broad valley beyond, halting at Echo City— most picturesque and bright of little villages, destined, perhaps, to realize its ambitious name some time in the remotest future.

The scene here is—as has been said in advance—a really pastoral one. The broad plain, left by the encircling mountains, is green and fresh; the river winds through its grassy expanse in pleasant quiet, without brawl or rush; the trees are like those in a familiar Eastern country-side. Only the great outlines of the surrounding hills, and here and there the appearance on the horizon of some sharper, higher, more distant peaks, show the traveller his whereabouts, and take his mind from the quieter aspect of what lies about him. Near by, in valleys leading into this, are various Mormon settlements; for we are already in the country of the saints.

But the grandest gorge is still to come; and the road enters it almost at once after crossing the little plain. It is Weber Cañon—the greatest of these Utah ravines. Its immense walls are grander by far than those of Echo; the forms of their ragged edges and the carvings of their surfaces are more fantastic; and the deep, dark aspect of the whole narrow valley gives in every way a nobler scene. It should be viewed on a cloudy, gloomy day, to realize its whole look of wild grandeur. The little river brawls at the left of the track; the thunder of the locomotive echoes from the high precipices at its sides; the rush of the train's onward motion adds a certain additional wildness to the shadowy place.

The old emigrant-road passes through the cañon, like the railway. It crosses and recrosses the river, and winds among the trees along the banks, sometimes lost to view from the train. Little frequented as it is in these days, the writer has seen, within a very few years, a "prairie schooner" of the old historic form passing along it; a rough, strong emigrant riding beside it; children's faces looking out between the folds of the cloth covering; and household goods dimly discernible within. And at one of the river-crossings is a mark that must often have given renewed hope or pain to many a one among this family's predecessors—the famous old "Thousand-Mile Tree," that stands at just that weary distance from Omaha, even farther from the great city by the Golden Gate.

DEVIL'S GATE, WEBER CAÑON.

Whoever follows the nomenclature of Weber Cañon would be led to think the enemy of mankind held there at least undisputed sway. All the great glories of the view are marked as his. The Devil's Gate—a black, ragged opening in one part of the great gorge, through which the foaming waters of the river rush white and noisy—is one, but it is well named. A very spirit of darkness seems to brood over the place. On each side, the broken cliffs lie in shadow; the thundering water roars below; there is no verdure but a blasted tree here and there; great bowlders lie in the bed of the stream and along the shore. In the distance, seen through the gap, there are black hills and mountain-summits overlooking them. And there is a cool wind here, that is like a breeze blown across the Styx, and that is never still, even in the hottest summer day.

Devil's Slide, Weber Cañon.

It is worth the while to think, in this wonderful valley, of the engineering skill that was needed to carry the iron road through its depths. All through the cañon are evidences of the difficulties of the task. Here a truss-bridge and web-like trestle-work carry the rails from one point of the rocky wall to another beyond the stream; here, for a great space, the road-bed is cut from the very sides of the great cliffs, where the gorge narrows and leaves no room for more than sand and river. And, as if to mock at it all, Nature has tried her hand, too, at construction, with a success at once weird, sublime, and grotesque. On the left hand of the route,

TERRES MAUVAISES, UTAH.

Salt Lake.

on the steep front of the rocky cliff, appears at one point the very mockery of human work—the singular formation called " The Devil's Slide "—by that same rule of nomenclature that we have mentioned once before. Two parallel walls of stone, extending from summit to base of the precipice, and enclosing between them a road - way, regular and unobstructed. An editor, whom your guide-books will be sure to quote, has written a good, though somewhat too statistical, description of this singular place ; we have found it in a well-used route-book, and quote it, in default of words that could say more :

" Imagine," the writer says, " a mountain eight hundred feet high, composed of solid, dark-red sandstone, with a smooth and gradually ascending surface to its very pinnacle, and only eight or ten degrees from being perpendicular. At the foot of this mountain the Weber River winds its devious course. From the base of the immense red mountain, up its entire height of eight hundred feet, is what is called 'The Devil's Slide,' composed of white limestone. It consists of a smooth, white stone floor from base to summit, about fifteen feet wide, as straight and regular as if laid by a stone-mason with line and plummet. On either side of this smooth, white line is what appears to the eye to be a well-laid white stone-wall, varying in height from ten to twenty feet. This white spectacle on the red mountain-side has all the appearance of being made by man or devil as a slide from the top of the mountain to the bed of Weber River."

This odd freak of Nature has nothing sublime about it; the whole idea that it conveys is that of singularity; but it is strangely picturesque and striking.

And now we are nearing the very centre of Mormondom; for only a little beyond the Devil's Gate, which, though first named, is farther toward the western extremity of the cañon than the "Slide," we come to Uintah Station, glance at the Salt-Lake Valley, and are hurried on to Ogden, whence the trains go out to the City of the Saints itself. Ogden lies in the great plain of the valley, but from the low railway-station you see

Plains of the Humboldt.

in the distance long ranges of mountains, more picturesque than almost any distant view you have had thus far; and all about the town are green fields—yes, positively fenced-off fields—and beyond them the prairie; but here no longer without trees.

Whoever will may leave this station—a great central point of the line, for here the Union and the Central roads meet and cause the dreary business of changing cars —and, adding a day or two to his journey, may take the sonorously-named Utah Central Railway—as if, indeed, the Territory boasted a net-work of iron roads—and journey down to Salt-Lake City to see the curious civilization he will find there. "It lies in a great valley," says the statistical and accurate description of this city of the Mormons— a description which we prefer to partly set down here rather than to run risks of error by trusting our own memory for any thing more than picturesque aspects—"it lies in a great valley, extending close up to the base of the Wasatch Mountains on the north, with an expansive view to the south of more than one hundred miles of plains, beyond which, in the distance, rise, clear cut and grand in the extreme, the gray, jagged, and rugged mountains, whose peaks are covered with perpetual snow." (Oh, unhappy writer in statistical guide-books! How much more "grand in the extreme" is that view in its bright reality than any words of yours or mine can show to those who have not seen it! Let us keep to our statistics.) "Adjoining the city is a fine agricultural and mining region, which has a large and growing trade. The climate of the valley is healthful, and the soil, where it can be irrigated, is extremely fertile. . . . The city covers an area of about nine miles, or three miles each way, and is handsomely laid out. The streets are very wide, with irrigating ditches passing through all of them, keeping the shade-trees and orchards looking beautiful. Every block is surrounded with shade-trees, and nearly every house has its neat little orchard of apple, peach, apricot, plum, and cherry trees. Fruit is very abundant, and the almond, the catalpa, and the cotton-wood-tree, grow side by side with the maple, the willow, and the locust. In fact, the whole nine square miles is almost one continuous garden."

So it will be seen that even a city on the Plains has elements that entitle it to a place in this record of the picturesque, and that it is not as other cities are. But Mr. Charles Nordhoff tells us, in his "California," that "Salt Lake need not hold any mere pleasure-traveller more than a day. You can drive all over it in two hours; and when you have seen the Tabernacle—an admirably-arranged and very ugly building—which contains an organ, built in Salt Lake by an English workman, a Mormon, named Ridges, which organ is second in size only to the Boston organ, and far sweeter in tone than the one of Plymouth Church; the menagerie of Brigham Young's enclosure, which contains several bears, some lynxes and wild-cats—natives of these mountains—and a small but interesting collection of minerals and Indian remains, and of the manufactures of the Mormons; the Temple Block; and enjoyed the magnificent view from the back of the city of the valley and the snow-capped peaks which lie on the other side—a view which you carry with you all over the place—you have done Salt-Lake City, and have time, if you have risen early, to bathe at the sulphur spring. The lake lies too far away to be visited in one day."

But, in spite of its distance, the great inland sea should certainly be seen. It is a remarkable sight from any point of view, and as you come suddenly upon it, after the long days of travel, in which you have seen only rivers and scanty brooks, it seems almost marvellous. A great expanse of sparkling water in the sunshine, or a dark waste that looks like the ocean itself when you see it under a cloudy sky, it is an outlook not to be forgotten in many a day.

Here, before we leave the Salt-Lake region, we must say a word to correct one very false idea concerning it—that which obtains concerning its great fertility and natural

PALISADE CAÑON.

wealth of soil. This point is referred to in Mr. Nordhoff's book, and, so far as we know, almost for the first time correctly; but we have never passed through Utah by the railway, or passed a day in this portion of the country, without greatly wondering why the common, unfounded theory had kept its place so long. It is popularly supposed that the Mormons have settled in a very garden of the earth, and that their Canaan was by no means all visionary; and there are not a few good people who have agitated themselves because these heathen had possession of one of the noblest parts of the American territory.

This is all entirely wrong. The region is really, by Nature, an arid desert, made up of veritable "Terres Mauvaises," though not such picturesque ones as lie, dotted with monumental rocks, but a little distance from the lake. The Mormons can truly boast that they have made their land "blossom like the rose;" but only by the greatest toil and care, and by an expenditure of wealth utterly disproportionate to its results. "Considering what an immense quantity of good land there is in these United States," says Mr. Nordhoff, "I should say that Brigham Young made what they call in the West 'a mighty poor land speculation' for his people. 'If we should stop irrigation for ninety days, not a tree, shrub, or vine, would remain alive in our country,' said a Mormon to me, as I walked through his garden. 'Not a tree grew in our plains when we came here, and we had, and have, to haul our wood and timber fourteen to twenty miles out of the mountains,' said another. The soil, though good, is full of stones; and I saw a terraced garden of about three acres, built up against the hill-side, which must have cost ten or twelve thousand dollars to prepare. That is to say, Young marched his people a thousand miles through a desert to settle them in a valley where almost every acre must have cost them, in labor and money to get it ready for agricultural use, I should say not less than one hundred dollars. An Illinois, or Iowa, or Missouri, or Minnesota farmer, who paid a dollar and a quarter an acre for his land in those days, got a better farm, ready-made to his hand, than these people got from Brigham, their leader, only after the experience of untold hardships (which we will not now count in), and of at least one hundred dollars' worth of labor per acre when they reached their destination." It will some time be more widely appreciated how completely the whole pleasant pastoral scenery here is the work of men's hands; for the present, the passage just quoted is so true that it shall serve as the only reference here to the subject.

West from Ogden lies the second great reach of the long overland journey. Salt-Lake City, an oasis of humanity, if not of a very high order of civilization, serves to mark the half-way point in the modern crossing of the Plains. The railways meet at Ogden Station, and the continued journey toward the western coast is made on "the Central," as the affectionate abbreviation of the railway-men calls the latter half of the great iron road. It passes westward through Corinne, a station which derives its life and prosperity chiefly from its communication with the Utah silver-mines, and reaches Prom-

Pleasant Valley, Truckee River.

ontory — properly, it seems,
called "Promontory Point,"
which appears a strange bit of tautology.
Here is a noteworthy place, and one which
all historians of the future ought to cele-
brate, each after his manner. Close by
the station, which the road reaches after skirting the shore
of the great Salt Lake for a little time, and then suddenly
curving away, the great iron line, pushed westward from the
east, met and joined that which for many months had grown
slowly toward it from the west—the last links of the iron
chain were riveted. There were jubilant ceremonies when
the great day of ending the road came at last, on the 10th of May, 1868. A rose-
wood "tie" joined the last rails; and solemnly, in the presence of a silent assembly,
a golden spike was driven with silver hammer—the last of the thousands on thousands
of fastenings that held together the mightiest work made for the sake of human communication and intercourse in all the world. The engines met from the east and west,
as Bret Harte told us—

> " Pilots touching—head to head
> Facing on the single track,
> Half a world behind each back "—

and there was a girdle round the earth such as the men of a century before had not dared even to dream of.

Beyond the memorable Promontory comes a dreary waste—the dreariest that has yet been passed, and perhaps the most utterly desolate of all the journey. Nothing lives here but the hopelessly wretched sage-brush, and a tribe of little basking lizards; yes, one thing more—the kind of gaunt, lank animals called "jackass-rabbits," that eat no one knows what on this arid plain. The horizon is bordered by bare, burned mountains; the ground is a waste of sand and salt; the air is a whirl of alkali-dust. Kelton, and Matlin, and Toano, dreariest of Nevada stations! Could any man wish his direst enemy a more bitter fate than to be kept here in the midst of this scene for a decade?

There is some mineral wealth, farther on, hidden near the route of the railway; but, apart from this, there would seem to be nothing useful to man obtainable from all this region. We dash across the sterile space in a few hours, but imagine for a moment the dreary time for the old emigrant-trains, which came on to these gusty, dusty levels in old days, and found neither grass, nor water, nor foliage, until they came to Humboldt Wells, blessed of many travellers, lying close together within a few hundred yards of the present road, and surrounded with tall, deep-green herbage. There are nearly a score of these grateful springs scattered about in a small area; and they are of very great depth, with cool, fresh, limpid water.

They herald the approach of another and a different district, for now we soon come to the Humboldt River itself, and for a time have all the benefit of the growth of trees along its sides, and the fertility that its waters revive along its course. The soil here is really arable; but go a little distance away from the river, and the few water-pools are alkaline, and the land resumes the features of the desert-soil. The scenery here, in the upper part of the Humboldt Valley, is for a time varied, and in many places even wild and grand. The road winds through picturesque cañons, and under the shadow of the northernmost mountains of the Humboldt Range, until the important station of Elko is reached. This is a noteworthy supply-station for all the country around it, in which are numerous mining settlements. The town is a place of great import to all the guide-books of this region. It has a population of more than five thousand, as we learn from one account of it; and there are a hundred and fifty shops of various kinds, great freight-houses, an hotel, two banks, two newspapers, a school, and a court-house. Truly a most promising prairie-town is this, to have grown up in three hurried years, and to flourish on the borders of a desert!

For now we have a little more of sage-brush and alkali, ant-hills, and sand. Let him who passes over the Humboldt Plains on a hot August day, and feels the flying white dust burning and parching eyes and mouth and throat, making gritty unpleas-antness in the water wherewith he tries to wash it away, and finding lodgment in every fold of his clothing, be sufficiently thankful that he is not plodding on with jaded

Truckee River, Nevada.

horse by the side of a crowded emigrant-wagon, with days of similar journeying behind him, and some of it still to come.

Emigrant or passenger by luxurious Pullman car, he will be glad to come near to the refreshing grandeur of scenery of the Palisades—though the finest of this is not seen without leaving the established route, and penetrating a little into the mountains at one side. It is here that you come upon such glimpses and vistas as the one Mr. Moran has drawn—breaks in the rocky wall, through which one looks out on really perfect mountain-pictures. There are hot springs here ; and in one valley a host of them sends up perpetual steam, of sulphurous odor, and the ground is tinged with mineral colors, as at the geysers of

California. All around us, too, are mining districts, some of them old and exhausted, some still flourishing. To the pioneers they all have association with "lively times;" the veterans talk of "the Austin excitement," and the famous "Washoe time"—periods which seem like a distant age to us.

The railway and the emigrant-road have long followed the course of the Humboldt River, but this is not always in sight after Battle Mountain—named from an old Indian combat—is passed; and finally it is lost to view altogether, and the road runs by the fresh, bright-looking little station of Humboldt itself; past Golconda, and Winnemucca, and Lovelock's, and Brown's—names that have histories; and finally Wadsworth is reached, cheerfully hailed as the beginning of the "Sacramento division," a title that reads already like the California names. And here the Plains are done—the Sierras fairly begin.

The monotony of the view begins to change; the mountains slope about us, as we enter the well-named Pleasant Valley, through which Truckee River flows, and at last, passing through well-wooded land again, reach Truckee itself, a little city in the wilderness, standing among the very main ridges of the Sierra chain. The town—the first of the stations within the actual limits of California—is a picturesque, bright place of six thousand inhabitants—a place that has had its "great fire," its revival, its riots, and adventures, not a whit behind those of the larger mining towns farther toward the interior of the State.

Along the rocky shores of its river lie the noblest scenes; the tall cliffs are ragged and bare, but pine-tree-crowned; the rock-broken water ripples and thunders through gorges and little stretches of fertile plain; and the buzzing saw-mills of an incipient civilization hum with a homelike, New-England sound on its banks. From the town itself, stages—the stages of luxury and civilization, too—carry the traveller to the beautiful and now well-known Donner Lake, only two or three miles away. The great sheet of clear and beautiful water lies high up in the mountains, between steep sides, and in the midst of the wildest and most picturesque of the scenery of the Sierra summits. The depth of the lake is very great, but its waters are so transparent that one can look down many fathoms into them; they are unsullied by any disturbance of soil or sand, for they lie in a bed formed almost entirely of the solid rock.

Few things could have more perfect beauty than this mountain-lake, and its even more famous neighbor, Lake Tahoe, some fifteen miles farther to the south. The scene is never twice the same. Though it lies under the unbroken sunlight through a great part of the summer weather, there is perpetual variation in the great mountain-shadows, and in breeze and calm on the surface. There is a climate here that makes almost the ideal atmosphere. It is neither cold to chilliness nor warm to discomfort, but always bracing, invigorating, inspiring with a kind of pleasant and energetic intoxication. Already invalids come to these saving lakes from east and west, and find new life up among the

DONNER LAKE, NEVADA.

pines and summits. There are trout in the waters around, and fishing here is more than sport—it is a lounge in dream-land, a rest in a region hardly surpassed anywhere on the globe.

Here, as elsewhere in the Sierras, the rock-forms are picturesque and grand at all points of the view. Castellated, pinnacled, with sides like perpendicular walls, and summits like chiselled platforms, they give a strangely beautiful aspect to every shore and gorge and valley. The road, twelve miles in length, by which Lake Tahoe is reached from Truckee, affords some of the most remarkable and memorable views of these formations, with all their singularities of outline, that can be obtained in any accessible region in this part of the range; and it would be impossible to find a more glorious drive than is this along the edge of the river-bed, over a well-graded path, through the very heart of one of the noblest groups of the Sierra chain. It is a ride to be remembered with the great passes of the world—with the Swiss mountain-roads, and the ravines of Greece—in its own way as beautiful and grand as these. The great cañons, and such noble breaks in the rock-wall as can give us glimpses like that of the Giant's Gap, and a hundred others, are certainly among the vistas through which one looks upon the chosen scenes of the whole world.

It has been said that the traveller is here in the very centre of the mountain-range. The general features of structure in this most noble region of the continent have been better described elsewhere than we can show them in our own words.

"For four hundred miles," says Mr. Clarence King, who knows these mountains, better, perhaps, than any other American, "the Sierras are a definite ridge, broad and high, and having the form of a sea-wave. Buttresses of sombre-hued rock, jutting at intervals from a steep wall, form the abrupt eastern slopes; irregular forests, in scattered growth, huddle together near the snow. The lower declivities are barren spurs, sinking into the sterile flats of the Great Basin.

"Long ridges of comparatively gentle outline characterize the western side; but this sloping table is scored, from summit to base, by a system of parallel, transverse cañons, distant from one another often less than twenty-five miles. They are ordinarily two or three thousand feet deep—falling, at times, in sheer, smooth-fronted cliffs; again, in sweeping curves, like the hull of a ship; again, in rugged, V-shaped gorges, or with irregular, hilly flanks—opening, at last, through gate-ways of low, rounded foot-hills, out upon the horizontal plain of the San Joaquin and Sacramento. . . .

"Dull and monotonous in color, there are, however, certain elements of picturesqueness in this lower zone. Its oak-clad hills wander out into the great plain like coast promontories, enclosing yellow, or, in spring-time, green, bays of prairie. The hill-forms are rounded, or stretch in long, longitudinal ridges, broken across by the river-cañons. Above this zone of red earth, softly-modelled undulations, and dull, grayish groves, with a chain of mining-towns, dotted ranches, and vineyards, rise the swelling middle heights

LAKE TAHOE.

of the Sierras—a broad, billowy plateau, cut by sharp, sudden cañons, and sweeping up, with its dark, superb growth of coniferous forest, to the feet of the summit-peaks. . . .

"Along its upper limit, the forest-zone grows thin and irregular—black shafts of Alpine pines and firs clustering on sheltered slopes, or climbing, in disordered processions, up broken and rocky faces. Higher, the last gnarled forms are passed, and beyond stretches the rank of silent, white peaks—a region of rock and ice lifted above the limit of life.

"In the north, domes and cones of volcanic formation are the summit, but, for about three hundred miles in the south, it is a succession of sharp granite *aiguilles* and crags. Prevalent among the granitic forms are singularly perfect conoidal domes, whose symmetrical figures, were it not for their immense size, would impress one as having an artificial finish.

"The Alpine gorges are usually wide and open, leading into amphitheatres, whose walls are either rock or drifts of never-melting snow. The sculpture of the summit is very evidently glacial. Beside the ordinary phenomena of polished rocks and moraines, the larger general forms are clearly the work of frost and ice ; and, although this ice-period is only feebly represented to-day, yet the frequent avalanches of winter, and freshly-scored mountain-flanks, are constant suggestions of the past."

There could not well be a more satisfactory, faithful, and vivid general characterization of the Sierra chain than this that we have quoted from the account of one of our greatest American mountaineers. Its faithfulness will be confirmed by every view, gained from whatever point, of the series of giant peaks that lie in long line to the north and south of our own special route through the range.

Far off from the railway-route, in those parts of the Sierras known as yet only to a few mountaineers, there is Alpine scenery, not only as grand as the great, world-known views in the heart of Switzerland, but even of almost the same character. Whoever reads Mr. King's "Ascent of Mount Tyndall" will find no more inspiriting record of mountain-climbing in all the records of the Alpine Club. Indeed, this range will be the future working-ground of many an enthusiastic successor of the Tyndalls and Whympers of our time, and the scene of triumphs like that of the great ascent of the before unconquered Matterhorn ; perhaps—though Heaven forbid !—the witness of disasters as unspeakably terrible as the awful fall of Douglas and his fellows.

In reading what Mr. King and his companions have written of the wonderful hidden regions of the great chain, which, for a time at least, we must know only through these interpreters, we, and every reader, must be particularly struck by one characteristic, which they all note in the scenes that they describe. This is the majesty of their desolation—the spell of the unknown and the unvisited. Mighty gorges, with giant sides, bearing the traces of great glacial movements, and watched over by truly Alpine pinnacles of ice and snow, are the weird passes into the silent region that surrounds the highest peaks

SUMMIT OF THE SIERRAS.

Giant's Gap.

within the limits of the United States. In the bottom of these deep cañons are lakes, frozen during the greater part of the year, and at other times lying with motionless water, never touched by canoe or keel.

Against the great precipices of the ravines are piles of *débris* such as are familiar to every traveller through the passes of the Alps. Snow, encrusted with an icy, brittle crust, lies heaped against other portions of the rocky walls, and crowns their tops.

High up, there are vast glacial formations; moraines, that lie in long ridges, with steeply-sloping summits, so narrow and sharp that it is almost impossible to walk along them. Here, too, are structures of ice, pinnacles and needles and towers, and sometimes piles which have formed against walls of rock, but have melted away until they are like great sheets of glass standing on edge, while through them a blue, cold light is cast into the chasm that now intervenes between them and their former precipitous supports. Almost every phase in the phenomena of Alpine scenery is repeated here—often with greater beauty than in that of Switzerland even, with which the very word "Alpine" has become so entirely associated by usage.

In this region of hidden grandeur lies the ground of hope for those cosmopolitan tourists who complain that the world is a small place, full of hackneyed scenes, after all. So long as there is locked up here in our great mountain-chain such a glory as the few who have penetrated into its fortresses have described, even the mountaineer who fancies he has exhausted two continents, need never despair.

One noble feature of the whole Sierra—of all of it save that which lies above the level of any vegetable life—is its magnificent forest-covering. It may well be doubted if the growth of forests of pine is ever seen in greater perfection than is found here. These tall, straight, noble shafts are the very kings of trees. Covering the great slopes with a dense mantle of sombre green, they lend a wonderful dignity to the peaks, as one looks upon them from a distance; and, to one already in the forest, they seem the worthy guardians of the mountain-sides. They are magnificent in size, as they are admirable in proportion. No mast or spar ever shaped by men's hands exceeds the already perfect grace of their straight, unbroken trunks. They are things to study for their mere beauty as individual trees, apart from their effect upon the general landscape, which even without them would be wild and picturesque enough.

Of all these features of the noble Sierra scenery, of which we have said so much, and spoken with such positive enthusiasm, the traveller by the railway sees little or nothing. For through the very finest regions of the mountains the track is of necessity

The San Joaquin River.

OAKS OF OAKLAND.

covered in by strong snow-sheds, extending, with only trifling breaks, for many miles. Indispensable as they are, no one has passed through their long, dark tunnels without feeling a sense of personal wrong that so much that is beautiful should be so shut out from view. Through breaks and openings he looks down into dark cañons, with pine-covered sides, and catches a glimpse of a foaming river hundreds of feet below, when suddenly the black wall of boards and posts closes in again upon the train, and the picture is left incomplete. That happiest of men, the lover of the picturesque who has the leisure to indulge his love, must not fail to leave the travelled route here for days, and to satisfy himself with all the grander aspects of what he will find about him.

The railway passes on from Truckee, climbing a gradual slope to Summit, fifteen miles farther, the highest station on the Central Pacific, though still lower than Sherman, of which we spoke long ago. Summit, standing at the highest point of this pass through the range, is at an altitude of seven thousand and forty-two feet above the level of the sea; and, to reach it, the track has ascended twenty-five hundred feet, say the guides, in fifty miles; and in the hundred and four miles between this and Sacramento, on the plain beyond, the descent must again be made to a point only fifty-six feet above sea-level.

This part of the journey—the western descent from Summit—is one that the writer has several times reached just at the most glorious period of sunrise. There can be no more perfect scene. The road winds along the edges of great precipices, and in the deep cañons below the shadows are still lying. Those peaks above that are snow-covered catch the first rays of the sun, and glow with wonderful color. Light wreaths of mist rise up to the end of the zone of pines, and then drift away into the air, and are lost. All about one the aspect of the mountains is of the wildest, most intense kind; for by that word "intense" something seems to be expressed of the positive force there is in it that differs utterly from the effect of such a scene as lies passive for our admiration. This is grand; it is magnetic; there is no escaping the wonder-working influence of the great grouping of mountains and ravines, of dense forests, and ragged pinnacles of rock.

But soon the mountains seem to fade away, and before we realize it we are among the foot-hills—those oak-clad or bare brown hills, that, as Mr. King told us in the passage we quoted, "wander out into the great plain like coast promontories, enclosing yellow, or, in the spring-time, green bays of prairie." And so out upon the plain of the San Joaquin. We might fancy ourselves back again upon the Plains were it not for the still farther range of heights before us. These are brown, bare, unpicturesque, outlying hills, and we dash through them by Livermore's Pass, having passed Sacramento, and go on our way toward the coast.

Civilization appears again; houses and towns begin to line the track; the stations are like similar places in the East; the prosaic railway-pedlers come back again with their hated wares; for us, the picturesque is over; and already the hum of the still distant city seems almost to reach our ears, as we dash in under the great green oaks of Oakland.

CHAPTER FIVE

The Yosemite
An artist's summer in Yosemite Valley

When did Yosemite secure its special niche in the American psyche? And how? This small but monumental granite-walled valley (and the park that surrounds it) has come to symbolize the preservation of wild places. It's a symbolic preeminence that some would claim is all out of proportion to Yosemite's real importance, real beauty, and the real wilderness character it still possesses after being admired almost to the point of destruction by generations (and millions) of visitors. But there it is. For better or worse — and I believe for better — Yosemite Valley has become synonymous with mountain beauty, drama, grandeur. Its cathedral-like, holiest-of-the-holy status serves as a kind of guarantee and rallying point for the defense of other wild landscapes; and even the most recklessly pro-development forces in the West, politicians and special interests, have learned their lesson and shy away from nibbling at the special and specially preserved character of Yosemite.

The myth of Yosemite — a myth which is as vital in the struggle to conserve American wilderness as the vacation-time reality of our most famous National Park — this myth has been a long time in the making. And here we're in at the very beginning: We visit a Yosemite before John Muir's advocacy really paid off, before the Sierra Club took up the torch, before Ansel Adams' images became an integral, acquired part of our national culture. These pages are among the first tidings — tell the people, the secret's out.

James D. Smillie, the author/illustrator, had neither the naturalist's passion of a Muir, or the draftsmanship of a Moran. But he's left us a fascinating account of a summer's sketching in the Yosemite Sierra. Certainly, we cringe at the blatant and contradictory racism of his account of the surviving Yosemite Indians. (Smillie ridicules them for living in brush homes, but goes into raptures when his trusty guide is clever enough to build such a brush shelter after a day on the trail!) But we delight in his painterly appreciation of High Sierra light, his constant discovery of new images, his artist's awareness of a Yosemite already in transition.

We're tempted, reading such an account, to congratulate ourselves on how dramatically our ideas and perspectives have changed in a hundred-odd years — how much more enlightened we are, how our capacity to care has grown, to care for people as well as the land. But really it's been a slow and uncertain sort of progress, two steps forward, one back; and in the intervening years a lot of what was wildest in the West has slipped through our fingers and disappeared. Nostalgia rather than self-congratulation may be a fitter response to a book like this. It was a grand time, this period after the explorers and before mass tourism; a grand time in a West that now exists, no longer even in memory, but only in books.

L.T-F.

THE YOSEMITE.

WITH ILLUSTRATIONS BY JAMES D. SMILLIE.

Half-Dome, from the Merced River.

THE journey from the Atlantic to the Pacific is a fitting introduction to the Yosemite, which most nobly crowns the grandest pleasure-tour within the limits of our country. Palace, drawing-room, sleeping, and hotel cars, do not suggest, in title at least, the weariness of travel; and the vast country traversed presents so great a variety of interest that all sense of monotony is banished, as, day after day and night after night, the sleepless engine rushes on, tireless.

Two days and a half, flying at railroad speed through fleeting landscape, with now and then a busy town or great, roaring city —two nights of hurrying sleep, and the journey from the Atlantic to the Missouri River is complete. The great plains of North America stretch away to the west, seemingly boundless as the ocean; a wild spirit of freedom breathes in the very air that pipes and whistles

106

through the train, in true nautical style, as the third night folds its dark curtains over these limitless wilds, and the sun of the fourth morning rises upon the same unbroken scene. Then come grand views of the distant Rocky Mountains, followed by the wonder-land of the Green-River country, where cliffs tower, wild and fantastic in form and color. Farther on, the grim walls of Echo, Weber, Devil's Gate, and Ogden Cañons, echo and reëcho the roar and thunder of the intruding train. The Wahsatch Mountains are passed, and the heavy waters of Salt Lake ripple and blaze, like burnished gold, in the light of the setting sun. On the morrow, barren, treeless mountains, alkali-desert, and sage-brush, reign supreme. Daybreak of the seventh, and last morning, gladdens the eyes with a sight of sturdy evergreen-forests. Now there is but a long downhill to the plains of California; the character of the forest-growth changes; herbage is scant, and the bare earth is red-brown; the air is hot, and has lost the exhilarating vitality of the morning, heat trembles over the plain, and soon the engine pants in the seething crowd at Sacramento. Once more under way, the barriers of successive folds of the Coast Range are passed; and, at the close of day, crossing the bay to San Francisco, the chill Pacific wind greets the Atlantic traveller, forcing him, with a shiver, to draw close the overcoat that at noon would have been insufferable.

The Yosemite Valley lies among the Sierra Nevadas of California, nearly in the centre of the State, north and south, and midway between the east and west bases of the mountains, at this point a little over seventy miles wide. In a direct line it is one hundred and fifty miles almost due east from San Francisco, but at present it can hardly be reached by less than two hundred and fifty miles of travel. The name is an Anglicized or corrupted form of the Indian A-hom-e-tae, which means Great Grizzly Bear, supposed to be the title of a chief, and applied generally to a tribe that held possession of the region from the valley to the plains on the west. That name, however, was never given it by the Indians. They call it A-wah-nee, which finds its equivalent in the Spanish cañon or the English chasm.

In 1851 the miners and early settlers on the Mariposa estate were driven to desperation by these thieving Indians. A military company was organized to operate against them, and, directed by Tenaya, a friendly red-skin, they followed the flying and astonished aborigines into their innermost hiding-place, the now famous Yosemite. It was then the turn of the white men to be astonished; and, when the company returned to the settlements, marvellous stories were told of what had been seen. This is the story of the discovery. The Indians did not lay their first lesson well to heart. They continued their depredations, and, in consequence, another expedition chased them from their stronghold the following year. They fled to the protection of a powerful tribe, the Monos, farther in among the mountains; were hospitably received by them, but betrayed their confidence, and, in return, were slaughtered almost to the last man. Reports vary, but it is generally agreed that less than half a dozen of the Yosemite tribe now survive.

BIG TREES—MARIPOSA GROVE.

It was not until 1855 that the first tourists' visit was made to the valley. Then a party went in, under the guidance of Mr. J. M. Hutchings. The same season a second party followed; next year a trail was completed on the Mariposa side, and regular pleasure-travel commenced. The same year (1856) the first house or shanty was put up; but to Mr. J. C. Lamon belongs the credit of being the first actual settler. He built a cabin, and yet lives there, alone, summer and winter.

In 1864 Congress passed an act fixing the boundaries, and setting apart, "for public use, resort, and recreation," the Yosemite Valley and the Mariposa Grove of Big Trees. The State of California was to appoint commissioners and assume the trust, which at once she did, and the people of the United States rejoiced in their grand park. Claims have been made based upon the rights of settlers to land in the valley, but the courts have decided adversely to them.

It was one morning in June, as bright as such mornings usually are, that our little party started for Yosemite. Taking cars on the Central Pacific Railroad, we returned east eighty miles to Lathrop, and then, on what is known as the Visalia Division, turned south, crossing diagonally the broad valley of the San Joaquin. The road is now finished, so that travellers may go almost to the foot-hills of the Sierras by rail. We trundled along in good old style, with a coach-and-six. The wheat-harvest was already being gathered, and nothing could be more foreign to Eastern eyes than the huge machinery, barn-like in dimensions, drawn by a score of mules, "heading" a swathe of at least fifteen feet wide. Every thing was in proportion to the vast fields, of thousands of acres each, that had to be worked over. The heads only of the wheat were cut off, the stalks being left for fertilization, or for the cattle that are allowed to range, fall and winter, over these fenceless plains. The exact line of our road seemed to be largely a matter of will on the part of our driver, for he drove wherever he pleased; no barriers prevented, and most of the grain had been cut. No tree, or bush, or living green thing, gave vitality to the landscape. Through a thin, tremulous haze, the forms of the Sierras in the east, and the Coast Range in the west, were faintly visible. The sky overhead was cloudless, a deep violet tint pervading, in strong contrast to the earth-tones of ochre and orange—a strange combination, blending duskily at the horizon, and in tint and tone calling to mind familiar pictures of Egypt, Syria, and the East. After several hours' riding, exposed to a fierce sun, the scene became monotonous, and by degrees very tiresome. At last the Sierra forms loomed up, distinct and near, inviting visions of breezy heights and refreshing forest shadows; but hours of disappointment followed, for, to the toil of climbing among the foot-hills, was added the loss of the breeze that blows regularly over the plains, even though it were a warm one. Already, at this season, the earth was browned; herbage was scant; ochre, umber, and sienna-tints prevailed; the leaves of the buckeye were falling, crisp and dry; dust covered the glossy green of the beautiful manzanita; the digger-pines stood samples of attenuation; and, over all, pervading all, was a sentiment not so much of decay as desiccation. Hornitas, an irregular and uninteresting gathering of buildings, was passed; and, from the heights beyond, the plains could be seen stretching in luminous obscurity. Very gradually the barrenness gave place to chaparrals of oak, manzanita, and chamiso; and trees clothed the crests of the mountain-spurs, after the manner of forests. At last we reached Mariposa, about thirty miles from the plains by the road we travelled, and calling to memory only a dusty, hot street; low, shabby-looking brick buildings; and surrounding hills, that were without any compensating wildness or beauty to excuse them for standing as barriers to the longed-for breezes. Here the forests began to assume a more familiar appearance, as oaks and evergreens clustered in denser growth. Ten or fifteen miles farther on, at an elevation of more than three thousand feet, the timber was superb. Coniferous trees preponderated, different varieties of oak being next in importance. Compared with Eastern-State forests, there is very little undergrowth, the woods having a singularly open appearance, and showing to great advantage the noble sugar- and pitch-pines, many of which are more than two hundred feet high, and from seven to ten feet in diameter. It might be fancied that, in forests where trees attained such proportions, there would be majestic solemnity, sylvan recesses, depths profound, and what not. On the contrary, an air of cheerfulness reigned, as the sunshine, streaming through, lighted into bright, warm

Fallen Sequoia.

color the shaft-like trunks of pitch-pine and cedar. At Clark's Ranch, more than fifty miles from the plains, the carriage-road ends, but it has been surveyed and partially completed into the Yosemite. Here, then, the scant baggage was to be transferred to the backs of mules, and the remaining twenty-four miles done in the saddle; but, before going on, it is usual to spend a day among the big trees of Mariposa, four miles distant, but not in the direction of the Yosemite.

The grant of the Mariposa Grove covers four sections, or two miles square, and is under the charge of the Yosemite commissioners. The first that was known of the big trees was in the spring of 1852, when a hunter discovered what is now called the Calaveras

Bridal-Veil Fall.

Grove. He could get no one to believe his story, and had to resort to a trick to get any of his companions to go with him to the trees, so as to verify his statements. Once verified, descriptions were widely published, and, from San Francisco papers, copied into English prints. In 1853 an English botanist published a scientific description, and designated the tree as the *Wellingtonia gigantea*. In 1854 an eminent French botanist, M. Decaisne, at a meeting of the " Société Botanique de France," presented specimens of the big trees and redwood that he had received from the consular agent of France at San Francisco. He explained at length his reasons for considering the big tree and redwood as belonging to the same species, *Sequoia*, an affinity the English botanist had overlooked; so, in accordance with the rules of botanical nomenclature, the new species was called *Sequoia gigantea.* Professor Whitney, State Geologist of California (upon whose faithful work I have drawn liberally), says: "It is to the happy accident of the generic agreement of the big tree with the redwood that we owe it that we are not obliged to call the largest and most interesting tree of America after an English military hero. Had it been an English botanist of the highest eminence, the dose would not have been so unpalatable." (Sequoia, it will be remembered, was the name of the Cherokee Indian who, early in this century, invented an alphabet and written language for his tribe.) So far as is yet known, there are but eight distinct patches or groves of the big trees. They are very limited in range, and seem to belong exclusively to California. They form groves, largely intermixed with other trees, very little below five thousand and never over seven thousand feet above sea-level. They have been, without difficulty, largely propagated from the seed, and fine specimens are now growing in many parts of America and Europe. A few miles south of the Mariposa Grove, the *Sequoias* seem to find a more congenial home, and may be found of all ages and sizes, from the seedling up. A mill, at this place, saws them into lumber. Professor Whitney closes his very interesting chapter by saying: "The big tree is not that wonderfully exceptional thing which popular writers have almost always described it as being. It is not so restricted in its range as some other coniferæ of California. It occurs in great abundance, of all ages and sizes, and there is no reason to suppose that it is now dying out, or that it belongs to a past geological era, any more than the redwood.

"The age of the big trees is not so great as that assigned by the highest authorities to some of the English yews. Neither is its height as great, by far, as that of an Australian species, the *Eucalyptus amygdalina*, many of which have, on the authority of Dr. Müller, the eminent government botanist, been found to measure over four hundred feet." The tallest *Sequoia* that has been measured is in the Calaveras Grove, being three hundred and twenty-five feet high, overtopping Trinity-Church spire (a standard of height familiar to most New-Yorkers) by forty feet. The greatest in diameter is the "Grizzly Giant" in the Mariposa Grove, which measures thirty-one feet through at the ground, and twenty feet at eleven feet above the ground. Clarence King described one that he saw in the forest some miles south of Mariposa, "a slowly-tapering, regularly round column, of about forty feet in diameter at the base, and rising two hundred and seventy-four feet." A very large tree in the Calaveras Grove, twenty-four feet in diameter, was, after much labor, cut down, and the base, at six feet from the ground, was smoothed and prepared as a dancing-floor; thirty feet farther up, the trunk was again cut through, and the rings, marking the growth of each year, were carefully counted. Upon this evidence, after making allowances and calculations, Professor Torrey pronounced the tree about thirteen hundred years old. It is not likely that any now standing are much older.

The ride from Clark's Ranch to the grove is less than four miles; so, after an early breakfast, we started for a day of picnic and sketching. The trail was well worn and easy, the air gloriously pure, and the forest delightful. It would be useless to attempt to describe the confusion of sentiment and impatience that possessed me as I rode along, peering anxiously through the labyrinth of the wood for the first glimpse into the vast portals of that grand old grove. Memory recalled the solemn gloom of a hemlock-forest among the Catskill Mountains—if that was dark, then surely this must be savage— if that was solemn, then this must be awful! To me, the sighing of summer breezes through those high tops would be the ghostly echo of wild storms that had done battle with them for hundreds of years. Inarticulate with the lore of dead ages, their moans would breathe the sad history of centuries past; their towering heads, with scarce perceptible nod, would tell of Goths and Vandals that scourged Europe when they were young; of King Arthur and "his table round," while yet they were in the vigor of early maturity; and of Mohammed and his wars, written upon the page of his-

tory, before their limbs creaked with age. They might whisper something of lost races on this continent, or of the advent of the red-man; to them Columbus would be a matter of yesterday, and our dear Revolutionary War a scarce noticeable thing of to-day.

The guide shouts, " There is a big tree!" What! are we so near

Valley Floor, with View of Cathedral Spires.

the sacred precincts? Where is the atmosphere of awe? where the elements that were to hush the voice, and fill the whole being with reverential exaltation? Alas! there was the first big tree, sunlight sparkling all over its great cinnamon-colored trunk, and I was ready to shout, and, spurring my prosaic beast, to rush with the rest in a graceless scramble to be first to reach his majesty's foot. The charm was broken. I was willing, anxious to be deeply moved, but no answering emotion came—such moods do not come at the bidding. Unsought, they have welled up since at thought of that day—but not then; no, not then. I had built an ideal grove, and at first sight it was demolished, but that was no fault of the Mariposa big trees. There was no gloomily grand grove, there were no profound recesses; the great trees stood widely apart, with many pines and firs interspersed, and sunlight streamed down through all and over all. I wandered about, sorely disappointed that they did not look bigger, and yet every sense told me that they were vast beyond any thing that I had ever seen; and it was not until after I had been among them for hours, and had sketched two or three, that their true proportions loomed upon my understanding. Then I wondered at the practical man who was "pacing-off" the diameter of the "Grizzly Giant," and at the woman of little faith, who had brought with her a piece of twine to verify the oft-told story of size. It is hardly possible to form a just idea of size or height until, getting at a distance where the whole tree may be seen, a mounted figure takes position at the base, thus establishing an initial point for computation. In form they are often savagely gaunt, their respiratory apparatus of foliage being in remarkably small proportion to their tower-like trunks. The bark is very light and fibrous, like the outer sheath of a cocoa-nut, of a singular cinnamon-color, and running in great ridges that vary from ten inches to three feet in thickness. Some trunks appear quite smooth, but others are warted and gnarled as though wearing the wrinkles of great age. The Indians and sheep-herders have been accustomed every year to burn the undergrowth through the woods, and by this practice, now strictly prohibited, most of the trees in the Mariposa Grove have been injured, a few but slightly; but, in many cases, soundness and beauty have been seriously impaired. On an area of thirty-seven hundred by twenty-three hundred feet there are just three hundred and sixty-five *Sequoias* of a diameter of one foot or over, but not more than twenty are over twenty feet in diameter. Two or three, greater than any that stand, now lie prone and broken; the trail lies through the hollow section of one that has fallen and been burned out. An ordinary-sized man, sitting upon a horse, can but just touch with his knuckles the blackened arch overhead.

The afternoon, rich in contrasts of glowing lights and broad shadows, too quickly followed the inquisitive glare of noonday sun; pictures in effect and color presented themselves where, an hour before, there had been only a confusion of petty forms, sharp and shadowless, under the almost perpendicular rays of sunlight; the novelty of first acquaintance was wearing off, and the true grandeur of proportions was developing with

CATHEDRAL SPIRES.

fascinating rapidity. The spirit was groaning within me that pencil and color in my hands were so weak, when through the hush came the faintest mutterings of distant thunder. The rest of the party had gone, and with them the picnic element. I was alone, and the booming of the rapidly-nearing storm, as its echoing waves of sound rolled through the pillared forest that seemed to stand dumbly expectant, was to me the grand original, of which grimly-solemn cathedral and deepest organ-note are but a type. Threatening clouds darkened the sky, a few great drops of rain adding emphasis to the warning. Hastily gathering my scattered scraps, I retreated, but not without a last, hungry, devouring look. Now there is pictured in memory a mighty shadowed forest, its branches moving uneasily, and sighing as the storm sweeps torrent-like through it.

As has been already stated, Clark's Ranch is the present end of the carriage-road, and the beginning of the bridle-path into the Yosemite, which is only twelve miles distant in a direct line, although nearly twice that by the trail. Its altitude is about four thousand feet, being a little higher than the floor of the valley, but between it and the valley lies an elevation that must be crossed, which is about three thousand five hundred feet in height, nearly equal to the average of the Catskill Mountains, the highest point reached in crossing being seven thousand four hundred feet above the sea. Here are barns and stables, a saw-mill, and several long, low, irregular one-story houses, with characteristic arrangement of verandas, upon which open all the doors and windows, there being no passages or hall-ways in the buildings. Guides, hunters, and dogs, loiter about; horses wait in groups, saddled and bridled; uneasy travellers flit from house to house, and an air of business generally possesses the place, in spite of the close, hedging, heavy timber, that brings the air of the primeval wilderness to the very doors.

Our scant luggage was securely packed for the ride, and early in the morning the horses were brought out—a dejected-looking lot, each with a rope-halter about its neck, giving more the appearance of so many candidates for the gallows than toilers for a pleasure-party. It was interesting to watch the packing of the load upon the mule's back, the curiously-intricate cording and strapping, and then the final binding of beast and burden into one inseparable mass. Two strong men laid hold of the ropes, the passive mule between them, and pulled as though striving each to outdo the other. Could toughened hide or bony framework resist? The brute made no sign. They placed each a foot against the pack, and their weight was added to their muscle for one final effort; a faint ugh! came from the stolid creature, and a crunching sound, as of a great egg-shell in collapse, told me that my sketch-box had come to grief; but no matter, there was no time to stop for trifles; a heavy hand took hold upon the top of the pack, vigorously shook it—the mule vibrated as though it were part and parcel. "He must get out of his skin before he can get out of that," said the guide, and he was started on the trail.

It is not necessary to go all the way to the Yosemite to enjoy the picturesque effects of a party of pleasure-seekers, *en route*. The gay colors that inevitably find place, the grouping, action, light and shade in constantly-changing combination with the surrounding landscape, are a never-failing source of pleasure. Now, in bright sunlight, every spot of color tells with intensest power against a mass of sombre green; again, in the deep shadow of a wood, they form yet deeper shadows, and their richer color darkens

Sentinel Rock and Fall.

against the light beyond. Crossing an open space, how a white horse with red-shirted rider puts a climax upon all that there is of light and color; or, straggling over an upland waste of blinding-white granite-sand, how invaluable to the picture the strong relief of the black mule and his grotesque pack! So we spent the morning, crossing streams and climbing hill-sides, thankful for the cool, fragrant shadow of dark pines, and rejoicing

Sentinel Rock from the North.

in the light of broad meadows brilliant with flowers, and opening into long vistas hedged with close - standing fir - trees. Now and then a broad waste of rock had to be passed, and several times, from heights, we had views of the high Sierra peaks. It was soon after noon when we reached Paregoy's, a cattle-ranch and half-way house. Meadows, covered with natural grasses, following the course of running streams, stretched for miles in narrow belts, where great numbers of horses and cattle roamed and found pasture. We were surprised by a remarkably good dinner, although the request for a boiled egg could not be complied with—twenty minutes of trying proved an utter failure; we were a little over seven thousand feet "up in the world," where eggs do not observe the "three and a half minute" rule as they do upon lower levels. It was not long before we were again mounted and on the way, impatient to get over the five miles that intervened between us and Inspiration Point. If, the day before, we rode in the excitement of expectation, it was intensified now; every step brought us nearer to a place that hitherto had been to me like some crater in the moon or spot on the sun. There was no doubt as to its existence, but it belonged to the realm of fancy, now to be transferred to the real —a change almost dreaded. It is dangerous work to force our ideals from fancy to fact.

from poetry to prose. I knew it, and these questions were constantly repeated: Was grim disappointment waiting? were the senses to be benumbed on that dizzy height? would every line and every color harmonize to produce an effect overwhelming? At last, through the trees, there gleamed a pale, mist-like whiteness—it must be a wall of rock—could that be the first sight into the valley? The pulse quickened, the hard saddle and the shabby shamble of the offending beast underneath were forgotten, as he forced himself into quicker gait in answer to impatient drubbings; a few moments more, and we rode out to a clear space under pine-trees, where every evidence was presented of the many feet that had halted there before us; so, following their indications, and the unmistakable suggestions of our prosaic beasts, we alighted, and fastened them to well-

worn branches of pine or manzanita. A few yards only of *chaparral* intervened between us and the cliff—a rush and a bound—in a moment our feet were upon Inspiration Point, and— Mr. Clarence King, for whose descriptive powers I have great admiration, says: " I always go swiftly by this famous point of view now, feeling somehow that I don't belong to that army of literary travellers who have here planted themselves and burst into rhetoric. Here all who make California books, down to the last and most sentimental specimen who so much as meditates a letter to his or her local paper, dismount and inflate."

Warned by the lateness of the hour, and that we had yet

Rock Slide.

seven miles to ride before we could reach the nearest house, we again mounted our horses, and commenced the descent, nearly three thousand feet in three miles, over a very tortuous trail, rocky or dusty by turns, extremely tiresome to the wearied body, but never dangerous, there being no cliffs or precipices such as formed the grand picture constantly before us. Pine-trees, more or less dense, sheltered the way; and the scenery was enough to lift any one, not hopelessly dead or unobservant, far above the petty discomforts of saddle or trail. Every change of position presented some new charm—trees grouped into picturesque fore-grounds, finding bold relief in light and shade against the opal and amethyst tints of distant granite cliffs; flowers nodding in the breeze that brought refreshment to the brow and music to the ear; and little streams dimpling and gurgling across the trail, as if un-conscious of the terrible leaps that must be taken before reaching the river below. In strong contrast to this living, moving beauty, beyond all, the walls, towers, and domes of the Yosemite rose grand, serene, impassive, broadly divided into tenderest shadow and sweetest sunlight, giving no impression of cold, implacable, unyielding granite, but of majesty, to which our hearts went out as readily as to the flowers and brooks at our feet. As we approached the level of the valley and the open meadows, the groves of trees and the winding river were more distinctly seen—the glorious, park-like character of the place presented itself. Why not cultivate carefully these natural beauties—make lawns of the meadows, trim out the woods that the different trees may develop their fullest form, and control the river's course with grass-grown banks? At last, the foot of the descent was reached, and away we cantered in the evening shades, the black-oaks lacing their branches overhead. Trees, bending in graceful framework, enclosed various pictures, one of the most charming being a view of the Bridal-veil Fall as it sprung over the wall nine hundred feet high. Its upper part sparkled a moment in the sun-light, a solid body; then, as though wrestling with invisible spirits, it swept into a wild swirl of spray that came eddying down in soft mists and formless showers. Emerging from the wood, a broad meadow lay before us; and high over all projected, far up against the eastern sky, the Cathedral Rocks, with buttresses cool and spires aglow. At their foot the river crowds so close that the trail is forced to find its way through a wilderness of great granite blocks, that lie embowered in a forest which has grown since they were hurled from their places on the cliffs above. Then followed a long level, and groves of pine and cedar. After the fatigue and excitement of the day, it was like entering a sanctuary, the spirit of the place was so solemn and full of rest. There was no sentiment of gloom, but rather of deep, slumberous repose; the thick carpeting of sienna-colored pine-spindles that covered the ground hushed each foot-fall; the pillared tree-trunks formed vistas that stretched, like "long-drawn aisles," to profoundest forest-depths; the branches, "intricately crossed," did not obscure the luminous sky above, or hide the tall cathedral-spires that burned ruddy in the last gleam of day; refreshment and invigoration were in the very atmosphere; with thankfulness, my whole being drank deeply, and, when in the gray of evening the hotel was reached, I was cool, calm, and—very hungry.

The first week after our arrival was spent making acquaintance with the more common points of interest and attraction. At first, submitting to the guides, we rode in beaten paths, and wondered and admired according to regulation; but, after a day or two, such bonds became irksome, and we ranged at will, there being really no need of a guide in an enclosure six miles long and at most but a mile and a half wide—no need of any one to direct attention to what the eyes could hardly fail to see, or the senses discover for themselves; and, then, it was so much more delightful to wander un-directed and unattended, on horseback or on foot, regardless of conventional ways, and yielding unreservedly to each new enjoyment. We soon knew each meadow and the separating groves of trees, every stream and every ford across the river. Within the limits we ranged there are but eleven hundred and forty-one acres of level bottom, according to government reports—a surface only about one-third greater than that of the Central Park of New-York City—and of this seven hundred and forty-five acres are meadow, the rest being covered with trees and *débris* of rock. From Tenaya Cañon, at the upper end of the val-ley, to Bridal-veil Creek, near the lower end, four and a half miles in a direct line, the decline is only thirty-five feet. Naturally enough, a surface so nearly level is very widely overflowed during the high water in the spring,

Foot of Sentinel Fall

caused by melting snows among the mountains beyond. The meadows are covered with coarse, scant grass; and innumerable flowers, generally of exceeding delicacy, find choicest beds in slight depressions, where the water lies longest. Through these meadows the Merced River winds from side to side, during the summer an orderly stream, averaging, maybe, seventy or eighty feet in width, the cold snow-water shimmering in beautiful emerald greens as it flows over the granite-sand of the bottom. Its banks are fringed with alder, willow, poplar, cotton-wood, and evergreens; upon the meadow-level are grouped, in groves more or less dense, pines, cedars, and oaks, the latter often bearing large growths of mistletoe; upon the rock-talus, mingling with the pines and firs, the live-oak is a distinctive feature; higher, and clinging in crevices and to small patches of soil, the pungent bay and evergreen oak form patches of verdure. From the foot of Sentinel Fall an excellent view may be had of the meadows, the groves, the river, and the slopes at the foot of the walls of rock on either hand. On the right is El Capitan, three thousand

three hundred feet high; on the left are the Cathedral Rocks, nearly two thousand seven hundred feet in height—the two forming what may be called the southern gate to the valley. Each of our illustrations, it is intended, shall present some characteristic feature of the valley. The opening cut was selected from many similar views at the upper end of the valley, where the pine-trees come down to the river's edge, and are mirrored in the still pools. Washington Column, more than two thousand feet high, stands out on the left, casting an afternoon shadow well up on the flank of the

Yosemite Fall and Merced River.

Half-dome, whose summit is almost five thousand feet above the river, or nine thousand feet above the sea. The distant view of the spires may serve to tell the story of the broad, tree-covered levels, so charming for scampers on horseback, and of the prisoning walls that are without suggestion of imprisonment. The spires are forms of splintered granite, about five hundred feet in height, and altogether not less than two thousand feet above the valley. Sentinel Rock combines more of picturesqueness and grandeur, perhaps, than any other rock-mass in the valley, its obelisk-like top reaching a height of over three thousand feet, the face-wall being almost vertical. The view from the north is taken from a point about midway between the foot of Yosemite Fall and Washington Column; the other is from a point as far south of it, presenting an entirely different aspect, its stupendous proportions dwarfing into littleness every thing at its base. The fall at the right, as shown in the illustration, exists only in the spring, as it depends entirely upon the melting snow for its supply. That its force and volume at times must be terrific, is evident from the gorge that it has hollowed at its foot. It is rarely that such exhibitions of destructive energy can be found. The climb up this water-torn gully ends all dreams of a well-ordered park below. Torrents pour into the valley as soon as the snow begins to melt, leaping the cliffs with indescribable fury, carrying immense rocks and great quantities of coarse granite-sand, to work destruction as they spread their burden over the level ground. In some places, this detritus has been deposited to the depth of several feet in a single spring. The air then is filled with the roaring of water-falls; the greater portion of the valley is overflowed; and the wayward Merced cuts for itself new channels, making wide waste in the change. At such times, the Yosemite Fall is described as grand beyond all power of expression. The summit of the upper fall is a little over two thousand six hundred feet above the valley; for fifteen hundred feet the descent is absolutely vertical, and the rock is like a wall of masonry. Before this, the fall of water sways and sweeps, yielding to the force of the fitful wind with a marvellous grace and endless variety of motion. For a moment it descends with continuous roar; in another instant it is caught, and, reversing its flight, rises upward in wreathing, eddying mists, finally fading out like a summer cloud. The full-page illustration is taken from a clump of pine-trees so near that, by the rapid foreshortening, the entire fall appears in very different proportions from those seen from the opposite side of the valley. Such a glimpse is given in the illustration " Indians bathing."

In the spring, water is an element of destruction, in freezing as well as in thawing. The little rills that filter and percolate into every crack and crevice of rock by day, as they freeze at night, enable the frost to ply its giant leverage; and, when disaster from water seems to threaten every thing, there is added the shock of falling cliffs. The granite-walls are not homogeneous in structure, some portions being far less durable, under the action of time and the elements, than others. The Half-dome and El

Indians making Chemuck.

Capitan are magnificent masses, at whose feet the *débris* are comparatively slight; but that part known as the Union Rocks, between the Cathedral and Sentinel Rocks, has suffered very much from disintegration. Great cliffs have fallen, and avalanches of rock have ploughed their way down the slope to the bottom of the valley. While climbing in such surroundings, the wreck of some world is suggested, so vast the ruin and so pigmy the climber. No words can convey other than a feeble impression of the effects of mountains of granite, sharp and fresh in fracture, piled one upon the other, the torn fragments of a forest underneath, or strewed about, as though the greatest had been but

Horse-Racing.

as straws tossed in the wind. A broad track of desolation leads away up to the heights from which these rocks have been thrown.

The attention may be diverted from cliffs and torrents to the human element characteristic of the place, poor though that element be, and in the change find much that is interesting in the few Indians that straggle, vagrant and worthless, through the region. They seem to be without tribal organization, although they still have "pow-wows," where their leading men, conscious of the inevitable decay of the race, strive to reorganize them and arouse their dying spirit; but the red-men are now hopelessly debauched and demoralized. In general appearance, they are robust, and even inclined to be fleshy; this latter is accounted for by the fact that acorns, their staple of food, are extremely fattening. There were at times as many as fifty Indians of all descriptions, male and female, old and young, living in the valley in the most primitive fashion, their "wallies," or huts, consisting only of branches stuck into the earth in semicircular form, the leaf-covered boughs meeting overhead. Generally they are dirty and disagreeable; but their voices are sweet, and their language is really musical. That some Indians do wash, I have had ocular demonstration; they are not all unqualifiedly dirty. While sitting at work on the river-bank, three young squaws came along and surprised me by deliberately preparing for a bath, not a hundred feet from me. They disported themselves with all the grace of mermaids, diving, swimming, and playing for nearly an hour in the cold snow-water. They stole a Chinaman's soap, and used it lavishly; and, making their fingers do duty as tooth-brushes, they showed a purpose of cleanliness as well as of sport. It was really a charming picture — the water so clearly transparent; the beach shelving in smooth slopes of sand; the trees overarching the stream; beyond all, the Yosemite Fall swaying in silvery showers, and, in the foreground pool, these children of Nature playing, their tawny skins wet with water and glistening with all the beauty of animated bronze. After their bath, they favored me with their company. One pulled from its place of concealment a Jew's-harp, and my ears were regaled with "Shoo, Fly!"

This particular bend of the river proved to be a place of regular Indian resort; for, on another day, within a few yards of my chosen ground, there was an encampment of not less than half a dozen squaws, more young ones, and yet more dogs. A fire was burning on the slope under the cottonwood-trees, and in it were a number of stones of small size. A circular basin, about three feet in diameter, and very shallow, had been carefully made in the fine sand, and into this acorn-flour was spread to the depth of three or four inches. The acorns are dried in the sun, hulled, and pounded between stones. By this rude process a very fine-looking, white flour is produced, but it is very bitter, and unfit for use until prepared. Conical baskets, of very fine osier, and filled with water, are made to stand securely by planting them in the sand. Into them hot stones are dropped, and in a few moments the strange spectacle is presented of a basket of water boiling violently. This scalding water is poured through cedar-boughs, held fan-like over the flour, until the sand-basin is full; it drains rapidly through; the process is repeated several times, until, on tasting, the flour proves to be sweet, the bitterness having all been leached away. The pasty mess is then scooped with the hands into one of the large baskets, mixed very thin with water, and into this gruel hot stones are dropped until it boils; it is stirred and cooked until about the consistency of mush, then it is considered good to eat. Up to this stage I had been intently watching, and seemed to interest the savages quite as much as they interested me. One of them, with a very limited stock of English, was evidently quite willing to use it for my benefit. I was invited to join them as they squatted about a large basket of *chemuck*, as they call it, which I did very readily. In addition to the chemuck, they had cooked, by the aid of hot stones, a very bitter weed, steeped it in water until it was tasteless, and that was now brought to add cheer to the festive scene. The youngest and most cleanly-looking squaw sat next to me, and made herself very agreeable by her aboriginal pleasantry and savage politeness. The old squaws were dirty beyond measure; they grinned as they ejaculated their gutturals, and seemed as willing to be agreeable as the younger ones. They honored me especially with a separate basket, holding maybe a quart of their acorn-gruel. I was desirous of tasting their preparation, even after having noted that all the water used was from the river in which the half-dozen or so of little Indians were making commendable efforts to get clean, marked by an unwillingness to duck and dive anywhere but in the very pools from which the cooking-supplies were drawn. But my nerves were strong and my purpose was stout to share the hospitality so kindly extended. The greens were put down by the chemuck, and the trial commenced by my red friend taking a quantity of the dripping greens, squeezing them dry in her hand, and offering them to me with pantomimic invitation to eat. With the quart of gruel in my lap and the squeezed greens in my hand, at the supreme moment I was any thing but hungry. They waited: I put the basket-bowl to my lips; they shook their heads, and their faces said that was not regular; my face asked what was the polite Indian manner. My kind friend promptly answered by first filling her mouth with greens, then dipping her four fingers into my gruel, ladling up a quantity, and then, with surprising quickness, transferring the half of her hand into her mouth. Further details are unnecessary. Up to this moment my stomach had remained passive; now it rebelled. I nibbled timidly at the greens, and dipped one finger into my chemuck. A shout warned me that that would never do, and again my red lady-friend set me an example, drawn from my private basket. I offered two, three fingers; they smiled derisively and shook their heads. The children and the dogs gathered around, and watched me with the wistfulness so peculiar to them. The situation was getting serious, so, with quick resolve and desperate energy, I plunged the half of my hand into the bowl; then, with a rapid twisting movement, tried to get it and the adhering gruel into my mouth. What a mess! Heart and stomach failed me, and my face told of complete discomfiture. With

YOSEMITE FALL.

one guttural grunt and a peculiar grimness of expression, the entertainers turned to help themselves with all the spirit and appetite so wanting in their guest. All dipping into one dish, it was an exciting race. The youngsters ladled out their share, and the dogs were not behind, enjoying, as they did, the advantages of direct communication, without the drawback of hands. What was not eaten at once of the chemuck was again cooked until very thick, then dipped out into a small basket, and turned into the cold water of the river, in such manner as to harden and take the form of old-fashioned "turnovers." They really looked inviting as they lay, white and rounded, in a pool at the river-side. In this form they are fit for use for a number of days. Chemuck is flat and tasteless; there is no salt used in cooking, but, to take its place, there is plenty of gritty sand. The sun went down behind Wa-haw-ka; the baskets and bread were gathered up, packed into the large cone baskets in which all loads are carried, strapped upon the backs of the oldest squaws, and they filed away, leaving their kitchen and banqueting-hall with no other trace of the day's work than the smouldering fire and the pits in the sand.

Hardly less nomadic or vagabond in character than the Indians were those rough fellows that found their way into the valley as mule-men, pedlers, and all those other nondescripts that are to be found hovering between the lines of civilization and the outer world of lawlessness. To such the grand excitement of the place was horse-racing, and the time invariably on Sunday. Any thing that looked like a horse might be a racer, and as great a tempest of excitement could be raised over a scrub of a mustang as though it were a thorough-bred. One Sunday morning I strolled to the upper end of the valley; a quiet like that of languor filled the air; the roar of the Yosemite Fall had died out, and now but a slender stream down the face of the cliff marked its place. In the hush I walked under the pine-trees, whose pendulous branches and long, tremulous needles vibrated into an Æolian melody upon the slightest provocation; a scarcely-perceptible breeze brought whispers, to be caught only by the attentive ear, that swelled through faultless crescendos into volumes of harmony, rich and deep, yet ever sounding strangely far away. From the shadows and music out to the sunlighted meadow was but a step. At the other extremity of the open space, four or five hundred yards away, was a group of men. Drawing nearer, it was plain to be seen that they were intent upon the preliminaries of a horse-race. There were Indians, Chinamen, Mexicans, negroes, and very dark-colored specimens of white men. There was a confusion of tongues, through which came the clear ring of clinking gold and silver coin, for all were betting —many of them their last dollar. Several horses were getting ready for the race; the favorites were a sorrel and a roan, or "blue horse;" all were very ordinary animals, and without the slightest training. There were no saddles; the riders, stripped of all superfluous clothing, bareheaded and barefooted, rode with only a sheepskin or bit of blanket under them; over the drawn-up knees and around the horse's body a surcingle was tightly drawn, binding horse and rider into one. Judges, starters, and umpires, were

Merced Gorge.

selected and positions taken. The word was given; the horses plunged, started, "bucked;" again they started; again the sorrel bucked. An unlimited amount of profanity expressed the impatience of the crowd. The " blue horse " was now largely the favorite.

" Now, boys, don't holler when the horses 's comin'—'cos you know the blue horse might fly the track — then whar's yer pile ?"

"No ! don't holler"— "we won't holler !" went up in one unanimous shout.

At last they came— a cloud of dust, rattling hoofs, and frantic riders plying their whips right and left over the struggling brutes under them ; on they came ; the squatting crowd sprang to their feet, and up went one simultaneous yell ; on they came, the crowd capering, screaming, and "hollerin'," like so many madmen ; all alike infected ; the stoical Indian as well as the mercurial Mexican. " Now shet yer hollerin'," men of mercury, or, "whar's yer pile ?" The " blue horse" led, and, in a cloud of dust, all dashed by. It was a whirlpool of excitement, the stake being the vortex. Round and round they went ; shouts, laughter, and profanity— one wild, incoherent Babel—losers and winners alike indistinguishable. Their hot temperaments found the excitement they craved, and the losers were rewarded in its drunkenness. Yet another very different interest is to be found in the visitors who throng the valley. Probably not less than two thousand come and go between May and October of each year, and, without exaggeration, they may be said to represent every nation and class of people on the globe. For their accommodation there are three hotels, where excellent fare is to be had, all the difficulties of getting supplies being taken into consideration. An enterprising individual has opened a saloon, with a display of cut-glass and silver that is quite dazzling. A great mule, staggering under the slate-beds of a billiard-table, carried the heaviest load that has yet been taken into the valley; and plans were laid, that by this time may have been realized, for sledding a piano over the winter snow, to be added to the establishment. Here, too, is the telegraph-office, where a single telegraphic wire connects with the outer world. A fifth house has been built, or perched, fourteen hundred feet above the valley-bottom, on the small rock-level between the Vernal and Nevada Falls. The proprietors of these establishments hold them subject to leases granted by the Yosemite commissioners. The same authority also appoints a guardian of the valley, whose duty it is to see that the rules for the preservation of the trees and the prevention of wanton defacement are properly enforced.

The scenic effects of winter are described as wonderfully beautiful, the ice-forms about the falls being particularly interesting. No doubt in time it will be the fashion to make winter-excursions into the Yosemite, but for the present it is safe to advise that, if the visit cannot be made in May or June, it be deferred until another season, for later in the year, to the disappointment of losing some of the finest features in the scenery, are added the discomforts of heat, toil, and an all-pervading dust, that penetrates to the innermost recesses of one's baggage and being. The temperature of spring is delightful, but during summer the thermometer frequently stands as high as 96° and 98°, while on the plains it is away above 100°.

There are now no less than five trails over which a horse may get in or out of the valley: the Mariposa trail, passing Inspiration Point, and entering at the southern end; the Coulterville trail, that comes in at the same end, on the opposite side; a third trail, passing near Glacier Point, and entering at the foot of Sentinel Rock, about midway up the valley on its eastern side; a fourth one, passing through the Merced Gorge by the Vernal and Nevada Falls; and the fifth, through Indian Cañon, on the west side, north of Yosemite Fall. Over this last it is barely possible to get a horse, and it is very little used. On the Coulterville route travellers may ride in stages to the beginning of the descent, and at its foot may again take vehicles to the upper end of the valley—about four miles of level road—so reducing the horseback riding to but three miles. It is a mistake to think that the natural barriers—the walls surrounding—are impassable; there are many places where a bold climber could, without any great difficulty, surmount all obstacles.

The trail through Merced Gorge, after reaching the top of Nevada Fall, crosses the

TENAYA CANON, FROM GLACIER POINT.

stream and the southern end of the Little or Upper Yosemite Valley. This valley, more than two thousand feet above its famous neighbor, is one of the many great granite basins peculiar to this section of country. The bottom is a little more than three miles long, and is a pleasant succession of meadows and forests, through which flows the Merced River. The sides are not so much walls as smooth, bare slopes of seamless granite, ribboned with sienna brown bands from running water, and here and there breaking into those strange dome-forms so provocative of questions that as yet have received no answer.

Among our more extended excursions we planned one to this place, and, as we were to camp out for several days, our preparations were careful, and, on starting, our cavalcade was imposing. Five riders led; three pack-horses followed laden with hampers and blankets, each pack crowned with an inverted kettle or a broad frying-pan. After commencing the ascent, the way led through woods, close grown, and filled with a tangled undergrowth that, with all its rank vigor, was unable to overtop the great fragments of rock that strewed the forest. In places, the trail twisted from right to left in sharp zigzags, and was so exceedingly steep that the horse and rider upon the turn above seemed to be almost overhead. Within sight the river roared and tumbled in a series of cataracts. We left our horses under a great overhanging rock, in charge of the guide, to be taken up the trail to meet us farther on, while we climbed by a foot-path around the base of a magnificent cliff, and out, face to face with that beautiful sheet of falling water called the Vernal Fall. It is a curtain unbroken in its plunge of four hundred feet; on either side, the narrow gorge, drenched with spray and glimmering with rainbow-tints, is green with exuberant vegetable life. Climbing long ladders, we reached the top, to find a broad, basined rock and a lovely little lakelet sparkling in the sunlight. Farther on, we crossed a slender bridge, Wildcat Cataract flying underneath, just beyond which the little house already spoken of as between the Vernal and Nevada Falls found anchorage to the flat rock. Before us Nevada Fall came tumbling over a wall exceeding six hundred feet in height; to the right the Cap of Liberty, a singular form of granite, rose more than two thousand feet; all about were heights and depths, grand to look up to, terrible to look into. We had rejoined our guide and horses, and, passing through a clump of dark-looking firs that clustered at the foot of the Nevada Fall, we came out upon a slide of freshly-fractured, glistening granite that seemed impassable, but a way had been made, and up this avalanche of rock our horses betook themselves, climbing with wonderful pluck and sureness of foot. But one beast had shown a spirit of insubordination, so the guide had tied him close to a leader. At each angle of the zigzagging trail he would balk, refusing to follow; the other horse, keeping on regardless, pulled the obstinate creature into predicaments from which he could not extricate himself; then each pulled against the other, utterly indifferent as to consequences. In one of these contests the foothold of the leader gave way, and, in an instant, a confused mass of horse, an in-

General View of Yosemite, from Summit of Cloud's Rest.

extricable jumble of heads, legs, and tails, to say nothing of kettles and frying-pans, came bounding toward me; leaving the trail, the horses turned two or three somersaults among the broken rocks below, and then lay still. We clambered quickly down to them; they were not dead, did not even have any bones broken—their packs had saved them. One, lying wedged, with his feet in the air, received our first attention; ropes and straps were cut, and three of us undertook to roll the beast out of his position. No sooner did we get him to where he could use his legs, than he made one vehement effort, and we were tossed like children. I remember seeing a bald head, followed by a full complement of arms and legs, fly past me, as though projected from a catapult; the guide seemed to sink out of sight, and something, that struck very much after the manner of a trip-hammer, spread me on my back. In an instant we were upon our feet, to find that the horse had fallen upon the guide, who was lying under him pinned to the rock. Things now were really serious. Should the horse again struggle, the man under him would probably suffer fatal injury, so, another coming to the rescue, one sprung to the horse's head, holding it firmly down, while the other two, getting under the beast, lifted him bodily until the guide was able to drag himself out with nothing worse than a severely-sprained ankle and a bruised leg. It is not at all surprising that getting the horses on the trail proved much more difficult than their getting off. While the packs were being adjusted upon other horses, for these could barely hobble along, I made a sketch of the scene, looking down the gorge. In the distance is a glimpse of the western wall of the Yosemite. Nearer, on the left, is Glacier Point, rounding up to Sentinel Dome. The form to the right, in the middle of the picture, is a point called Crinoline, Sugar-Loaf, Verdant, and several other names. It is a spur from the shoulder of the Half-dome. The rock that forms the right of the sketch is a portion of the base of the Cap of Liberty. Resuming our way, we reached the upper valley late in the afternoon, and found an ingeniously-constructed, evergreen brush-house ready for us. It was short work to unpack and unsaddle our horses, turn them loose, gather wood, light a fire, and prepare our evening meal. During preliminary proceedings the two ladies of our party were engaged making gay and home-like the interior of our hut. Bright-colored blankets were spread with an eye critical to effect, and the heavy Mexican saddles made capital lounges and pillows. A stroll in twilight, until it deepened into moonlight, completed the day. In spite of all our precautions, the first night was really uncomfortable, owing to the cold; in the morning a gray rime of frost covered every thing; we were camping at an elevation greater than the summit of Mount Washington.

From camp we made an excursion to the top of Cloud's Rest, a point of view that surpasses all others in its comprehensiveness, as it rises at least six thousand feet above the Yosemite, or ten thousand above the sea. Starting after an early breakfast, we rode for an hour or two through open and scattered woods, climbing rapidly. Not very far from the summit we entered a remarkable grove of sugar-pines, through which ran a small stream, where grass grew abundantly. We took our horses to within a few hundred yards of the summit, after cantering over a waste of disintegrating granite, upon which stood, at wide intervals, strangely grotesque pines, gaunt of limb and thick-bodied, rigid and tendonous. Their branches were awry, as if suddenly stayed while wrestling for life against the storm, and their olive-brown verdure had no vital, sappy green to refresh the eye Upon the blinding whiteness of the rock and sand were traced, in severe lines, shadows more wild and weird even than the real forms, and over all stretched a vault of "dusky violet," completing a picture almost without suggestion of our familiar world of beauty. Here we left our horses and climbed to the top, which proved to be a long, thin, wave-like crest of granite, very narrow and piled with loose blocks that looked so insecure that it required steady nerves to walk its length, which in places was not more than ten or twelve feet wide. On the east side the descent was a steep sweep for hundreds of feet; on the west it was thousands. It fell away in one unbroken surface of granite, at an angle of not less than 45°, with no obstacle to stay a falling body until it should reach

the depths of Tenaya Cañon, at least a mile and a half distant. This slope is shown in the full-page illustration of Tenaya Cañon, where Cloud's Rest is the point just to the left of the Half-dome. It required some minutes to settle the nerves and look calmly about. To the north, over intervening cañons and gorges, the Sierra peaks rose grandly desolate, pale and delicately tinted with many tones, warm and cool, against the cloudless vacuum of the sky beyond, that, by contrast, wore a strangely sombre hue. Their shoulders were robed with snow and ice, and their flanks were grooved and scarred by glaciers long since extinct. Upon lower levels a sparse growth of evergreens hardly served to cover the naked appearance of the landscape, and bald spots of rock showed almost as white as

Gorge of the Merced, from Glacier Point Trail.

the snow beyond. This peculiar appearance of sterility, and meagre, patchy forest-growth, characterizes all the surrounding country when seen from such a height. Turning from the Sierras, that were from three to five thousand feet above our level, we looked down six thousand feet into the Yosemite, whose peculiar, trough-like formation was readily recognizable, running almost at right angles to the regular trend of the mountains, and fully four thousand feet below the average level of the surrounding country. The familiar

Half-dome.

forms of the enclosing walls, and the green groves and meadows of the valley - floor upon which the Merced sparkled, could be plainly seen, but angles of rock hid each water-fall.

No one can really claim to have seen the best general view of the Yosemite until he has climbed Cloud's Rest. In the illustration (p. 491) the form on the left, in light, is the Half-dome, of which views from different positions are presented : first, in the opening picture ; again, rising behind the figures in Horse-Racing ; in the full-page engraving of Tenaya Cañon ; from Glacier Point, and also from a point farther east, given on this page. Above it is Sentinel Dome, sloping down to Glacier Point ; a small bit of Sentinel Rock projects just beyond. Farther away are the Cathedral Rocks and Spires. Opposed to them, on the right, is El Capitan. Immediately underneath, in the picture, is the North Dome, sweeping down to Washington Column, and separated from the Half-dome by Tenaya Cañon. The Yosemite Fall is to the right, and back of the North Dome. The Gorge of the Merced, and Nevada and Vernal Falls, are to the left, and back of the Half - dome. Bridal - veil Fall is back of the Cathedral Rocks, away in the distance.

After a day or two we broke camp, and, by a new trail, over which we were the first to pass, made a *détour*, keeping along the upper edge of the Merced Gorge, crossing the Too-lulu-wack a few hundred yards above its fall, and thence to Glacier Point. This is one of the most interesting rides about the valley, presenting many grand and even startling views. From one point we could look down into what seemed a bottomless abyss, for it was impossible to see its greatest depth. Out of it came the roaring of distant waters and the lulling song of pine-tree forests. The Too-lulu-wack Fall was almost under us, and could not be seen ; but on the opposite side were the Vernal and Nevada Falls and the many cataracts of the Merced that, unlike most of the other streams that enter the Yosemite, are very imposing all the year round.

The Cap of Liberty rose prominently in the centre; back of that the upper Yosemite opened, and beyond all were the snow-capped High Sierras. In the engraving of this view, the peculiar rock-form and character of the upper valley walls or slopes have been quite lost. Passing on, we soon reached Glacier Point. At its northern end the Yosemite Valley divides in the form of a Y, Tenaya Cañon forming the left arm, and the Merced Gorge the right. Again, the Merced Gorge is divided like a T, the Merced entering on the left, the Too-lulu-wack on the right. Glacier Point is a spur of rock or mountain jutting out on the west or right-hand side of the valley, where it divides. From its terraced summit we looked down thirty-two hundred feet to the meadows at our very feet. Few can gaze into such a depth without a shudder. Directly opposite, on the other side, perhaps a mile and a half away, the Yosemite Fall came down half a mile in three leaps, its truly graceful proportions seen to greater advantage than from any other point. To the right, or north, we looked up Tenaya Cañon, its narrow floor beautiful with tall pines that almost hid its one jewel, Mirror Lake; but with walls grim and vast that swept on the right up five thousand feet to the grand, dominating form of the valley, the Half-dome. The bald slope and crest of Cloud's Rest towered beyond, and back of all the Sierras lifted their peaks, as yet untrodden by the foot of man. There can be but few places where so much of the terrible and the beautiful are at once combined.

From Glacier Point a trail leads to the summit of Sentinel Dome. Upon this height we spent an hour or more, enjoying already familiar features as viewed from a new stand-point. The ride thence to Paregoy's, distant about six miles, was through heavy forest. From Paregoy's we, brothers of the brush, returned to our old quarters in the valley, and worked hard for two months to bring away some limned shadow, however faint, of the wonders about us. At last our work was done, and our traps were packed for departure. Familiar with horses, pack-mules, and trails, we were independent of guides. The valley was filled with morning shadows when we started on our way. I led, dragging after me an extremely recusant pack-mule, that was pricked into conformity by G——, who followed, armed with a formidable stick, at least six feet long. Between our horses, the mule, and "last looks," much time was consumed, but Paregoy's was reached before one o'clock, and the late afternoon was spent trying to get a study of evening tints over the Sierras. The colorless granite is singularly responsive to certain atmospheric effects. Against a background of storm-cloud their forms stand wan and ghost-like; in the blinding glare of the mid-day sun they faint, almost indistinguishable; and, at sunset, they glow with a ruddy light, that is slowly extinguished by the upcreeping shadows of night, until the highest point flames for one moment, then dies, ashy pale, under the glory that is lifted to the sky above. Then the cold moon tips with silver those giant, sleeping forms, and by its growing light I cleared my palette, and closed the box upon my last study of the Yosemite and Sierras.

AFTERWORD:
The Sources of This Book

The five chapters comprising *Yellowstone to Yosemite* are all drawn from a single source, a remarkable source indeed, considering that in this reissue we have barely dipped into its over 800 pages of lavishly illustrated travel writing. The original book I'm speaking of was called *Picturesque America*, a kind of all-embracing travel encyclopedia of the United States as seen through late 19th-century eyes. This massive two-volume work, published in 1872, took the armchair traveler just about anywhere that the taste of the time deemed worth visiting.

Naturally, most of the picturesque spots that editor, William Cullen Bryant, thought worthy of a chapter were scenic destinations of the eastern seaboard. Places like Natural Bridge, Virginia, or the Delaware Water Gap, or Harpers Ferry. A few surprises slip in like Northern New Jersey, or Lake Mephrenagog; along with expected venues like Niagara Falls and the Catskills.

Not surprisingly, the West is seriously under-represented — we have reproduced most of the chapters on the West in this volume. The Spanish-American and Indian cultures of the Southwest that today's traveler considers the last word in really picturesque America are ignored completely.

Indeed, wherever native Americans appear in these narratives, they are treated with a high-handed scorn that makes the modern reader blush with shame. Such attitudes were seemingly the norm in that period. And in editing and preparing *Yellowstone to Yosemite*, I've left them, and all the original prose, untouched. Whether as a grim or as a quaint reminder of the way we were, I'm not quite sure. This book is a window into another world, another life, another West. I couldn't see filtering such a view through my own modern sensibilities.

It took me four years and a lot of frustrating correspondence with rare book dealers to discover an original copy of *Picturesque America*. A lovely piece of bookmaking in heavy, hand-tooled leather covers with exquisite marbled end papers. My motivation for this search was much more the beautiful illustrations than the interesting but dated prose. (It's humbling but healthy for a writer to realize that images age more gracefully than words.)

Most of the western illustrations in *Picturesque America* are by Thomas Moran, the celebrated middle brother of the Moran family of painters who, along with Albert Bierstadt, created a mythic West of grand vistas and transcendent stormy lighting that influenced the daydreams of generations... that still make us daydream. Thomas Moran, and the other two artists represented in this book, did not however physically create these fine wood engravings that bear their names. In the fashion of the day, these artists' sketches and paintings were transformed into line cuts by specialized technicians who would also sign the engravings (usually on the opposite side from the "artist's" name). Artists and engraving technicians — together they were magicians. And the West they gave us, half real, half imagined, is still working its magic.

Lito Tejada-Flores

PICTURESQUE AMERICA

PICTURESQUE AMERICA;

OR,

THE LAND WE LIVE IN.

A DELINEATION BY PEN AND PENCIL

OF

THE MOUNTAINS, RIVERS, LAKES, FORESTS, WATER-FALLS, SHORES,
CAÑONS, VALLEYS, CITIES, AND OTHER PICTURESQUE
FEATURES OF OUR COUNTRY.

With Illustrations on Steel and Wood, by Eminent American Artists.

EDITED BY WILLIAM CULLEN BRYANT.

PREFACE.

IT is the design of the publication entitled " PICTURESQUE AMERICA " to present full descriptions and elaborate pictorial delineations of the scenery characteristic of all the different parts of our country. The wealth of material for this purpose is almost boundless.

It will be admitted that our country abounds with scenery new to the artist's pencil, of a varied character, whether beautiful or grand, or formed of those sharper but no less striking combinations of outline which belong to neither of these classes. In the Old World every spot remarkable in these respects has been visited by the artist; studied and sketched again and again; observed in sunshine and in the shade of clouds, and regarded from every point of view that may give variety to the delineation. Both those who see in a landscape only what it shows to common eyes, and those whose imagination, like that of Turner, transfigures and glorifies whatever they look at, have made of these places, for the most part, all that could be made of them, until a desire is felt for the elements of natural beauty in new combinations, and for regions not yet rifled of all that they can yield to the pencil. Art sighs to carry her conquests into new realms. On our continent, and within the limits of our Republic, she finds them—primitive forests, in which the huge trunks of a past generation of trees lie mouldering in the shade of their aged descendants; mountains and valleys, gorges and rivers, and tracts of sea-coast, which the foot of the artist has never trod; and glens murmuring with water-falls which his ear has never heard. Thousands of charming nooks are waiting to yield their beauty to the pencil of the first comer. On the two great oceans which border our league of States, and in the vast space between them, we find a variety of scenery which no other single country can boast of. In other parts of the globe are a few mountains which attain a greater altitude than any within our limits, but the mere difference in height adds nothing to the impression made on the spectator. Among our White Mountains, our Catskills, our Alleghanies, our Rocky Mountains, and our Sierra Nevada, we have some of the wildest and most beautiful scenery in the world. On our majestic rivers—among the largest on either continent—and on our lakes—the largest and noblest in the world—the country often wears an aspect in which beauty is blended with majesty; and on our prairies and savannas the spectator, surprised at the vastness of their features, finds himself, notwithstanding the soft and gentle sweep of their outlines, overpowered with a sense of sublimity.

By means of the overland communications lately opened between the Atlantic coast and that of the Pacific, we have now easy access to scenery of a most remarkable character. For those who would see Nature in her grandest forms of snow-clad mountain, deep valley, rocky pinnacle, precipice, and chasm, there is no longer any occasion to cross the ocean. A rapid journey by railway over the plains that stretch westward from the Mississippi, brings the tourist into a region of the Rocky Mountains rivalling Switzerland in its scenery of rock piled on rock, up to the region of the clouds. But Switzerland has no such groves on its mountain-sides, nor has even Libanus, with its ancient cedars, as those which raise the astonishment of the visitor to that Western region—trees of such prodigious height and enormous dimenmensions that, to attain their present bulk, we might imagine them to have sprouted from the seed at the time of the Trojan War. Another feature of that region is so remarkable as to have enriched our language with a new word; and *cañon*, as the Spaniards write it, or *canyon*, as it is often spelled by our people, signifies one of those chasms between perpendicular walls ot rock—chasms of fearful depth and of length like that of a river, reporting of some mighty convulsion of Nature in ages that have left no record save in these displacements of the crust of our globe. Nor should we overlook in this enumeration the scenery of the desert, as it is seen in all its dreariness, not without offering subjects for the pencil, in those tracts of our Western possessions where rains never fall nor springs gush to moisten the soil.

When we speak of the scenery in our country rivalling that of Switzerland, we do not mean to imply that it has not a distinct and peculiar aspect. In mountain-scenery Nature does not repeat herself any more than in the human countenance. The traveller among the Pyrenees sees at a glance that he is not among the Alps. There is something in the forms and tints by which he is surrounded, and even in the lights which fall upon them, that impresses him with the idea of an essential difference. So, when he journeys among the steeps, and gorges, and fountains of Lebanon and Anti-Lebanon, he well perceives that he is neither among the Alps nor the Pyrenees. The precipices wear outlines of their own, the soil has its peculiar vegetation, the clouds and the sky have their distinct physiognomy.

Here, then, is a field for the artist almost without limits. It is no wonder that, with such an abundance and diversity of subjects for the pencil of the landscape-painter, his art should flourish in our country, and that some of those by whom it is practised should have made themselves illustrious by their works. Amid this great variety, however, and in a territory of such great extent, parts of which are but newly explored and other parts yet unvisited by sketchers, it is certain that no country has within its borders so many beautiful spots altogether unfamiliar to its own people. It is quite safe to assert that a book of American scenery, like "PICTURESQUE AMERICA," will lay before American readers more scenes entirely new to them than a similar book on Europe. Paintings, engravings, and photographs, have made us all, even those who have never seen them, well acquainted with the banks of the Hudson, with Niagara, and with the wonderful valley of the Yosemite; but there are innumerable places which lie out of the usual path of our artists and tourists; and many strange, picturesque, and charming scenes, sought out in these secluded spots, will, for the first time, become familiar to the general public through these pages. It is the purpose of the work to illustrate with greater fulness, and with superior excellence, so far as art is concerned, the places which attract curiosity by their interesting associations, and, at the same time, to challenge the admiration of the public for many of the glorious scenes which lie in the by-ways of travel.

Nor is the plan of the work confined to the natural beauties of our country. It includes, moreover, the various aspects impressed on it by civilization. It will give views of our cities and towns, characteristic scenes of human activity on our rivers and lakes, and will often associate, with the places delineated, whatever of American life and habits may possess the picturesque element.

The descriptions which form the letter-press of this work are necessarily from different pens, since they were to be obtained from those who had personally some knowledge of the places described. As for the illustrations, they were made in almost every instance by artists sent by the publishers for the purpose. Photographs, however accurate, lack the spirit and personal quality which the accomplished painter or draughtsman infuses into his work. The engravings here presented may with reason claim for "PICTURESQUE AMERICA," in addition to the fidelity of the delineations, that they possess spirit, animation, and beauty, which give to the work of the artist a value higher than could be derived from mere topographical accuracy.

The letter-press has passed under my revision, but to the zeal and diligence of Mr. Oliver B. Bunce, who has made the getting up of this work a labor of love, the credit of obtaining the descriptions from different quarters is due. To his well-instructed taste also the public will owe what constitutes the principal value of the work, the selection of subjects, the employment of skilful artists, and the general arrangement of the contents.

WILLIAM CULLEN BRYANT.